Sex Offenders
and Public Policy

Other Books in the Current Controversies Series

Sex Offenders and Public Policy

Lynn M. Zott, Book Editor

GREENHAVEN PRESS
A part of Gale, Cengage Learning

Detroit • New York • San Francisco • New Haven, Conn • Waterville, Maine • London

GALE
CENGAGE Learning™

Christine Nasso, *Publisher*
Elizabeth Des Chenes, *Managing Editor*

© 2008 Greenhaven Press, a part of Gale, Cengage Learning.

For more information, contact:
Greenhaven Press
27500 Drake Rd.
Farmington Hills, MI 48331-3535
Or you can visit our Internet site at gale.cengage.com

ISBN-13: 978-0-7377-3797-4 (hardcover)
ISBN-10: 0-7377-3797-2 (hardcover)
ISBN-13: 978-0-7377-3798-1 (pbk.)
ISBN-10: 0-7377-3798-0 (pbk.)

Library of Congress Control Number: 2001012345

Printed in the United States of America
2 3 4 5 6   13 12 11 10 09

ED105

Contents

Chapter 3: What Controversies Surround Sex Offender Policy?

Chapter 4: How Can Sex Offender Policies Be Improved?

The best method for reducing sexual assault involves promoting public safety with a combination of informed public debate, community education about child sexual abuse, community involvement, and the management of sex offenders in a way that targets those at highest risk for re-offending, encourages personal accountability, and reduces stressors that can discourage successful re-integration of offenders into society and lead to re-offending.

Foreword

By definition, controversies are "discussions of questions in which opposing opinions clash" (Webster's Twentieth Century Dictionary Unabridged). Few would deny that controversies are a pervasive part of the human condition and exist on virtually every level of human enterprise. Controversies transpire between individuals and among groups, within nations and between nations. Controversies supply the grist necessary for progress by providing challenges and challengers to the status quo. They also create atmospheres where strife and warfare can flourish. A world without controversies would be a peaceful world; but it also would be, by and large, static and prosaic.

The Series' Purpose

The purpose of the Current Controversies series is to explore many of the social, political, and economic controversies dominating the national and international scenes today. Titles selected for inclusion in the series are highly focused and specific. For example, from the larger category of criminal justice, Current Controversies deals with specific topics such as police brutality, gun control, white collar crime, and others. The debates in Current Controversies also are presented in a useful, timeless fashion. Articles and book excerpts included in each title are selected if they contribute valuable, long-range ideas to the overall debate. And wherever possible, current information is enhanced with historical documents and other relevant materials. Thus, while individual titles are current in focus, every effort is made to ensure that they will not become quickly outdated. Books in the Current Controversies series will remain important resources for librarians, teachers, and students for many years.

In addition to keeping the titles focused and specific, great care is taken in the editorial format of each book in the series. Book introductions and chapter prefaces are offered to provide background material for readers. Chapters are organized around several key questions that are answered with diverse opinions representing all points on the political spectrum. Materials in each chapter include opinions in which authors clearly disagree as well as alternative opinions in which authors may agree on a broader issue but disagree on the possible solutions. In this way, the content of each volume in Current Controversies mirrors the mosaic of opinions encountered in society. Readers will quickly realize that there are many viable answers to these complex issues. By questioning each author's conclusions, students and casual readers can begin to develop the critical thinking skills so important to evaluating opinionated material.

Current Controversies is also ideal for controlled research. Each anthology in the series is composed of primary sources taken from a wide gamut of informational categories including periodicals, newspapers, books, U.S. and foreign government documents, and the publications of private and public organizations. Readers will find factual support for reports, debates, and research papers covering all areas of important issues. In addition, an annotated table of contents, an index, a book and periodical bibliography, and a list of organizations to contact are included in each book to expedite further research.

Perhaps more than ever before in history, people are confronted with diverse and contradictory information. During the Persian Gulf War, for example, the public was not only treated to minute-to-minute coverage of the war, it was also inundated with critiques of the coverage and countless analyses of the factors motivating U.S. involvement. Being able to sort through the plethora of opinions accompanying today's major issues, and to draw one's own conclusions, can be a complicated and frustrating struggle. It is the editors' hope that Current Controversies will help readers with this struggle.

Introduction

It is a parent's nightmare: a son or daughter is abducted, sexually assaulted and murdered by a predator who had been lurking, undetected, in their community. This nightmare became a reality for the parents of Polly Klass, Megan Kanka, and Jessica Lunsford. The gruesome murders of these children brought about major changes in the prosecution and management of sex offenders who victimize children. Overwhelming public support for these changes began in the early 1990s and has continued, with many Americans expressing the belief that the prevention of sex crimes against children warrants and requires severe punishment of sex offenders. A 2005 Gallup Poll found that more Americans characterized themselves as "very concerned" about child molestation than about violent crime or terrorism.

The widely covered 1989 abduction of 11-year-old Jacob Wetterling and the 1993 kidnapping, sexual assault, and murder of 12-year-old Polly Klass led to the passage of the 1994 Jacob Wetterling Crimes Against Children and Sexually Violent Offender Registration Act, a federal law requiring states to maintain registries of sex offenders and other offenders who commit crimes against children. This law did not require states to make these registries available to the general public. In 1996, following the 1994 abduction, sexual assault, and murder of seven-year-old Megan Kanka by her neighbor, a twice-convicted sex offender, Congress passed Megan's Law. This legislation requires states to make information on sex offenders publicly available, if its law enforcement agencies deem that information necessary to protect the public. Also in 1996, the state of California intensified its punishment of sex offenders, ordering two repeat sex offenders to undergo chemical castration. Eight states presently allow either the chemical or surgical castration of convicted sex offenders.

In 2001 and 2002, a long history of sexual abuse of children by Catholic priests and church authorities' repeated failure to take action to prevent such crimes or punish priests who committed them was made public and dominated national headlines. The 2002 U.S. Conference of Catholic Bishops addressed this scandal by adopting large-scale efforts to prevent sex crimes against children, including mandating a curriculum to educate every church employee on the sexual victimization of children, and calling for severe consequences for priests who molest children.

The 2005 abduction, sexual assault, and murder of nine-year-old Florida resident Jessica Lunsford, who was buried alive by her neighbor, a registered sex offender, led to the passage of Jessica's Law in forty-three states between 2005 and 2006. Jessica's Law mandates stricter penalties for sex offenders who victimize children and requires lifetime tracking—by GPS (global positioning system) or other methods—of sex offenders classified as high risk. Residency restrictions are imposed on sex offenders in over half of all states, and in hundreds of cities; these restrictions prevent convicted sex offenders from living within a certain distance of schools, playgrounds, public parks, bus stops, or other areas where children gather. Some cities have even banned sex offenders from living anywhere within city limits. A few states have passed statutes allowing the civil commitment of sex offenders to mental health facilities for an indeterminate time period following their release from prison.

In 2006, President George W. Bush signed the Adam Walsh Child Protection and Safety Act, which mandated the maintenance of a national registry of sex offenders, greatly expanded the legal definition of sex offenses and sex offenders, and established Project Safe Childhood program within the U.S. Department of Justice. Project Safe Childhood includes grants to states to help combat Internet predators as well as to help fund civil commitments, and aims to coordinate federal, state, and local efforts to vigorously investigate and prosecute crimes against children, including sexual assault, child pornography, and kidnapping. Seven states have passed statutes that would allow the death penalty to be imposed in cases involving the sexual assault of a child. In 2003 a man in Louisiana was sentenced to death for the rape of his stepdaughter, and in 2007 the state Supreme Court upheld this conviction.

Although over eighty-five percent of sexual assaults on children do not involve abduction or murder and are committed by a trusted family member or an acquaintance with no criminal record, the public still links sexual assault with child abductions and murder, favoring harsher penalties over restorative options, such as community education and offender treatment. Opposition to punitive policies is often made on the grounds that they subject sex offenders to cruel and unusual punishment, thereby violating their constitutional rights. In addition, critics point to the fact that many of these measures target individuals who pose no threat to public safety, while other convicted criminals, including murderers, are not subjected to the restrictions that sex offenders face. Some warn that tougher laws can also have unintended negative consequences; severe restrictions on where sex offenders may reside, for example, often results in transient sex offenders who are difficult, if not impossible, to register or track.

These concerns, voiced by professionals in the field of sexual abuse, as well as law enforcement and civil rights activists, are often dismissed by the general public. Despite issues raised about the constitutionality, and unintended negative consequences of increasingly punitive and restrictive legislation aimed at sex offenders, these measures continue to garner popular support among the majority of Americans.

CHAPTER 1

Is Sex Offender Policy Based on Accurate Assumptions?

Chapter Preface

Since the mid-1990s, sex offender policy in the United States has become increasingly more punitive and restrictive. Anyone convicted of a sex crime—and the definition of what a sex crime is varies widely from state to state—is required to register as a sex offender. This person will have his or her personal details and crimes committed listed on Web-based notification sites for the remainder of his or her life, is likely to receive a longer sentence, and may have restrictions placed on where he or she can live, or be committed to a treatment center indefinitely following release from prison. The core belief that has driven these policy changes is that most children are sexually assaulted by strangers who are repeat offenders. Therefore, this argument follows, tracking and making public the whereabouts of known pedophiles and ensuring that they live and work as far away from children as possible will significantly reduce the sexual victimization of children.

This assumption has been strengthened, and as some have argued, perpetuated, by around-the-clock, high-profile media coverage of cases involving the violent deaths of children who were abducted, sexually assaulted, and murdered by previously convicted sex offenders living in their communities. These tragic stories compel an outraged and frightened public to urge their elected officials to pass laws to protect children from such dangers, and lawmakers respond enthusiastically. Laws are passed easily and with tremendous bipartisan political and public approval, and are often named after the children whose tragic deaths inspired their passage. Public support for these laws is based on the widespread perception that they are effective, based on sound, reliable, scientific research, and necessary to protect children against sexual victimization.

The core assumption that most children are sexually assaulted by strangers who are repeat offenders has not been supported by research. A statistical report published by the U.S. Department of Justice in 2000 revealed that only seven percent of offenders who sexually assaulted juveniles aged 0 to 17 were strangers to their victims; the vast majority—59 percent—of juveniles were assaulted by an acquaintance (e.g., a family friend, neighbor, babysitter, caregiver, teacher, coach, or religious leader), and 35 percent were assaulted by a family member. This report concluded that "this substantial component of America's crime problem"—the sexual assault of children ages twelve and under—"has been characterized by subjective assessments or atypical high profile crimes for too long." Furthermore, while some convicted sex offenders do go on to commit further offenses, statistics have shown that most of them do not, and the vast majority of perpetrators of sexual assault are acquaintances and family members with no prior record of sexual assault.

Those who argue that current policies are based on inaccurate assumptions about the perpetrators of sexual assaults against children are often quickly silenced by those who point to the horrific crimes committed by a few sadistic repeat offenders. According to Anna C. Salter, clinical psychologist and author of the 2003 book *Predators: Pedophiles, Rapists, & Other Sex Offenders*, 2 to 5 percent of sex offenders can be classified as sadists; nevertheless, attempts to reserve the harshest penalties for cases involving such offenders are viewed as being "soft on crime" or failing to "protect the children" by those who maintain that children are most likely to be assaulted by convicted criminals. Many experts agree that current sex offender policies—including registration, community notification, mandatory sentencing, civil commitment, and GPS (global positioning system) tracking aimed at convicted sex offenders—do nothing to protect children from the individuals who are most likely to sexually assault them.

Tougher Laws on Sex Offenders Increase Public Safety

George F. Allen

George F. Allen served as a Republican senator for the state of Virginia from 2000 to 2006. He was also the governor of Virginia from 1993 to 1998.

I rise this evening in strong support of the Adam Walsh Child Protection and Safety Act of 2006. I commend Senator [Orrin] Hatch for his steadfast leadership, his wisdom, and perseverance in finally getting this measure to the floor for a vote. It is long overdue.

I have always believed that one of the very top, most important responsibilities of government at the Federal, State, or, for that matter, the local level is the safety and security of our people, particularly the most vulnerable people in our society—our children.

When I was Governor of the Commonwealth of Virginia. I made the protection of the people of Virginia, including our children, our top priority. We worked with the legislature to abolish the lenient, dishonest parole system in Virginia that was releasing criminals after serving as little as one-fifth of their sentence. We instituted truth in sentencing in Virginia, and by doing that, when you read in the newspaper or see in the news that a felon has gotten a 20-year sentence, he is serving 20 years, not 4 or 5 years to come back out and prey upon innocent law-abiding citizens again.

Clearly, the abolition of parole, truth in sentencing, and longer sentences for felons has made Virginia safer. The crime rates are down, and there are tens of thousands of people who will not be victims of crime.

George F. Allen, "Children's Safety and Violent Crime Reduction Act of 2006," *Congressional Record—Senate*, vol. 152, no. 96, July 20, 2006, pp. S8017–S8018.

No Parole for Predators

I am going to talk about Adam Walsh, but there are a lot of other victims of crimes. I remember when we were trying to get the legislature and people behind the abolition of parole and truth in sentencing, listening to the stories of loved ones, of parents who would tell their stories, of people released early and where they have preyed upon, killed, or raped again.

If you look at the statistics . . . the highest recidivist rate, or the highest repeat offender rate of any crime . . . is [among] sex offenders.

I will always remember a lady talking about being raped, and then right after her, another woman was talking about being raped again, a second time, by that same person. That rapist was released early.

I remember talking about a police officer with young children. The police officer was killed on Father's Day in Richmond by someone released early. The story of a young person working in the bakery in Richmond who was killed by someone released early. The story of a mother talking about a violent assault and then the smothering with a pillow of her daughter, and then having to go back to the parole board to recount why that criminal, that murderer, should not be released once again.

Before I became Governor in Virginia, pedophiles were serving an average of 3½ years in prison. Now, with the abolition of parole, and truth in sentencing, their sentences are 26 years rather than 3½ years. Not surprisingly, there are now fewer victims of crime in the Commonwealth of Virginia. However, there continue to be child predators who lurk in the shadows of our society.

Most Sex Offenders Re-Offend

Studies show that there are more than 550,000 registered sex offenders in the United States, and there are an estimated

100,000 sex offenders who are missing from the system. Loopholes in this current system have allowed some sexual predators to evade law enforcement and place our children at risk. That is why the national registry aspect of this bill is so important.

Some may wonder, why is there such a focus on sex offenders? Why is there such a focus on pedophiles and sex offenders and rapists? The reason is, if you look at the statistics—and it is not unique to Virginia; it is the way it is across this country—the highest recidivist rate, or the highest repeat offender rate of any crime—even higher than murderers, even higher than armed robbers—is [among] sex offenders. That is why it is so important we have the registry. When someone is caught, first, they are getting a long sentence, and the best way to protect people is having these sex offenders behind bars rather than lurking in a parking garage or trying to lure young children. That is why the focus on sexual predators is so important, in that they have the highest repeat offender rate.

Now, these days, child predators have increased their ability to inflict harm on our children by exploiting new communications technologies, including the Internet. Please understand: I believe the Internet is the greatest invention since the Gutenberg press for the dissemination of information and ideas. It is a wonderful tool. And ever since I have been in the Senate, I have been working to make sure that avaricious State and local tax commissars don't impose 18-percent taxes on the Internet in monthly charges. We don't want the Internet monthly bills to look like a telephone bill. Ron Wyden from Oregon has been a good ally on this.

But the Internet also can create new opportunities for criminals, especially child predators. It is vitally important that we as parents and as elected leaders take the necessary steps to make the Internet as safe as possible for our children, as safe as possible for our children when they are at home, as safe as possible for them at schools, as well as in libraries.

Technology and Financial Incentives

I recently introduced a bill called the Internet Tax Nondiscrimination Act. This bill makes permanent the Internet tax moratorium, which is scheduled to expire next year. This measure also increases the ability of parents to protect their children from Internet predators. In fact, this is still law today. We want to keep this going.

This is vitally important, commonsense legislation that is going to protect and, indeed, it is going to save lives.

In our bill, we impose a responsibility on Internet service providers to offer customers filtering technology. The ISPs, or Internet service providers, need to limit access to material that would be harmful to minors. This feature will create a powerful, and does create a powerful, financial incentive for ISPs to provide the filtering technology that parents need. Once parents are empowered with this technology, I guarantee you they will use it to protect their young sons and daughters. I am pleased the Senate Commerce Committee approved this bill as part of the telecom reform bill on a vote of 19 to 3.

However, we as a legislative body have much more work to do, especially when it comes to increasing penalties on Internet predators, by giving law enforcement officials the tools they need to catch Internet predators and convict them. This is a key reason I have signed on as a cosponsor of the Adam Walsh Act. This legislation is vitally needed. As I said, it should have been passed many years ago. This legislation honors the memory of a 6-year-old boy named Adam Walsh who was kidnapped and murdered nearly 25 years ago. This bill also recognizes the tireless efforts of his parents, John and Reve Walsh, who have been outstanding advocates for children all across America, in making sure we have some common sense when we are combating violent criminals.

Stronger Internet Laws and Safety Provisions

The Adam Walsh Act—and I want to focus on one title—this bill in title 7 includes what is called the Internet Safety Act, sets out several provisions that will dramatically increase Internet safety, including tough new penalties for child exploitation enterprises and repeat sex offenders. This title also creates a new crime—and this is important—a new crime for embedding words or digital images on to the source code of a Web site with the intent to deceive a person into viewing this obscenity. This is vitally important for all people. I tell you, it is important for families and children. This section is going to help stop pornographers from tricking children into visiting their sites with words that are designed to attract innocent young people.

The Internet safety provisions in this measure also fund Federal prosecution resources, including 200 new Assistant U.S. Attorney positions to help prosecute persons for offenses related to sexual exploitation of children, and 45 more computer forensic examiners. These are the experts who will be helpful within the regional computer forensic laboratories in the Department of Justice. They include 10 more Internet Crimes Against Children task forces. These are also important. There is some good work being done in Bedford County, Virginia, in between Lynchburg and Roanoke. The sheriff, Mike Brown, in Bedford County has instituted Operation Blue Ridge Thunder which works on this, but the State and local folks can certainly use the assistance and help of the forensic experts and U.S. attorneys. After all, a lot of this is across State lines. All of these resources are absolutely necessary for the investigation and the prosecution of child sex offenses.

The Internet safety provisions in this bill also expand the civil remedy available to children who have been sexually abused and exploited.

This is vitally important, commonsense legislation that is going to protect and, indeed, it is going to save lives. It is perfect that we pass a bill named after Adam Walsh, a child who lost his life at age 6 to a child predator. It can be Adam Walsh, but to all the parents who are out there who lost a young child to a sexual predator, it can be their name put in here as well. The parents of Adam Walsh have dedicated their lives to making sure there are not other parents grieving with the loss of their son or their daughter. Adam's spirit lives on and the inspiration for action is in this measure, action that will save lives. More children will be able to grow up with the innocence they deserve and the safety they deserve, thanks to the efforts of Adam Walsh's parents and also the wisdom, on a bipartisan basis, of the Senate not to dawdle, but to act. I commend the Senate for acting, particularly those in the committee. I am honored to be a cosponsor, and I look forward to the passage of this act, the signing by the President, and the protection of children all across America.

Tough Laws and Vigilant Prosecution Are the Best Defense Against Sexual Predators

Alberto R. Gonzales

Alberto R. Gonzales served as the U. S. Attorney General from 2005 to 2007, and served as counsel to President George W. Bush from 2001 to 2005.

My favorite time of the day is when I tuck my sons in bed. I hold them and ask if they're doing ok, I hear their prayers and kiss them goodnight I try to listen carefully to what they say and study how their eyes light up when telling a story. Sometimes we laugh. These are magical moments for any parent. Life feels pure and sweet and everything seems possible. The breadth of a child's imagination and the depth of their dreams knows no limits in those twilight conversations.

But the morning dawn pulls back the curtains and reveals a harsher reality. A child's innocence is under siege every day from images, sounds, movies and music. And by far the greatest threat is the one posed by sexual pedophiles and predators. We are here today to discuss what else can be done to protect our children from these cowardly villains, who hide in the shadows of the Internet.

I know that you are already doing a lot to safeguard the innocence of our children through Project Safe Childhood. Thank you and God bless you

Now I am going to ask that you and I do more ... because quite honestly, what we are presently doing is not enough. It is not enough for us to become educated about child exploitation. It is not enough for us to be sickened. It is

Alberto R. Gonzalez, "Prepared Remarks of Attorney General Alberto R. Gonzales at the Project Safe Childhood Conference," December 4, 2006. www.usdoj.gov.

not enough for us to condemn. This is a national problem, requiring a national dialogue and creative thinking

Zero Tolerance for Predators

I think it is time to take Project Safe Childhood to the next level by asking that all of its partners—everyone here in this room today and your colleagues back home—join together in building a foundation for a national, zero-tolerance attitude towards pedophiles and sexual predators.

If there is evidence that a child has been hurt, I want to see an arrest, a thorough investigation and a merciless prosecution.

As a society, we already share a revulsion for what these criminals do to our children. The crimes are so terrible, that people are uncomfortable talking about them.

But if we are to make real progress, if we are to really stop pedophiles and predators before they strike, we need to move our country past revulsion and on to determination fueled by outrage, and finally on to action by parents, community organizations, law enforcement and victims groups. It is now your responsibility to inspire everyone in your communities to face this brutal threat with the same boldness that you do.

I have a vision for Project Safe Childhood that will make it the foundation on which we will build a national, zero-tolerance culture.

Today, I wish to share that vision with you . . . and I will ask for your help because no man or woman can do this alone.

First, to put it in the simplest of terms, we need to get pedophiles and predators off the street.

This means being aggressive in the cases you bring—show the world that there is no gray area when it comes to hurting kids.

We must transform ourselves before we can transform America into a place where children's safety is a guarantee.

We must therefore train ourselves so that no lead will ever cross the threshold of a U.S. Attorney's Office, local police precinct or advocacy center without some kind of follow up and action. If there is evidence that a child has been hurt, I want to see an arrest, a thorough investigation and a merciless prosecution if you have the evidence.

I know this is a tall order. It's asking you to pour even more blood, sweat and tears into this work than you already do—and what you already do is a lot.

But if we work together we can make it happen Remember—that's the structure that Project Safe Childhood has given you.

Cooperation Is the Key to Success

As I have said before, I see Project Safe Childhood as a strong, three-legged stool: one leg is the federal contribution led by United States Attorneys around the country, another is state and local law enforcement, including the outstanding work of the Internet Crimes Against Children task forces funded by the Departments Office of Justice Programs and the third is non-governmental organizations, like the Financial Coalition Against Child Pornography and the National Center for Missing and Exploited Children [NCMEC].

It's clear that cooperation is working—and we're going to make it work even better.

We must embrace the strength of this structure. We must talk to each other. Brainstorm and be creative. And go after these criminals with the full force of our laws

Second, once we get them off the street, we need to keep the pedophiles and predators behind bars.

We must seek stiff penalties for these criminals. If your state penalties are more aggressive, it should be a state-level case. If the federal law will put a pedophile behind bars for longer I want it to be a federal case.

Again, when we work together, we can make that happen. I've seen it. Under the Project Safe Childhood structure, state, local and federal partners are getting creative and seeking the toughest sentences possible. We have seen some great examples of this.

I'm very pleased to be able to announce today some additional funding that will help you make tough sentences a reality. We're making half a million dollars available for a Project Safe Childhood program—a program that will bring state and local law enforcement together with federal prosecutors from their regions. We are determined to equip law enforcement with all the knowledge they need so that they can work their cases and present them to our U.S. Attorneys' offices when necessary. When state and local law enforcement can work as easily with federal prosecutors as they already do with their district attorneys, a major obstacle to genuine cooperation will be overcome. Constantly expanding our ability to work together quickly and effectively is what Project Safe Childhood is all about

The training program will be kicked off at the NCMEC headquarters in early 2007 and, thereafter, delivered around the country.

Because I don't want just a few great examples of cooperation. I want it to be the standard operating procedure for everyone involved in PSC [Project Safe Childhood], nationally.

I am also interested in taking advantage of the mandates that Congress has given us on this issue.

We've had outstanding support from Capitol Hill over the past six years. They've given law enforcement additional tools to remove this blight from our neighborhoods

For example, I will support the development and implementation of new regulations for the Bureau of Prisons to pursue the civil commitment of mentally abnormal or disordered sex offenders who would pose a serious danger to others if released. Congress has been creative; they've given us the right to pursue that path and others like it, and we are going to. We're already implementing a number of other mandates that were included in the Adam Walsh Act. For example, I'm proud to say that the President just appointed Laura Rogers to be the Department's first SMART office coordinator. With her appointment, the Sex Offender Sentencing, Monitoring, Apprehending, Registering and Tracking Office will now be able to get to work on numerous important functions relating to the sex offender registry. Improving that registry, and giving the requirement to register some teeth was a creative step that is going to help all of us protect America's children.

Cooperative law-enforcement work on the registry has already led to some great stories of success. The first case brought under the Adam Walsh Child Protection and Safety Act involved a fugitive who was arrested by the Social Security Administration for allegedly using a false name and another man's Social Security number as he tried to set up a new identity for himself. It turns out that this individual was convicted for assaulting a police officer and possession of sexually exploitive material in Idaho in 2003 and he was wanted on a probation violation in another state for failing to register as a sex offender. He had done so at his first address, but did not re-register when he moved and then fled the state

Deputy U.S. Marshals—working with the Social Security Administration and the local U.S. Attorney's office—built a case against the man, and he was charged via criminal complaint for failing to register as a sex offender. The charges were brought in October [2006], making his the first case charged under the new act.

It's clear that cooperation is working—and we're going to make it work even better.

Raise Awareness and Teach Prevention

The third, and potentially most important step we all need to take to achieve this zero-tolerance vision is old-fashioned communication—raising our voices, together, to raise awareness and teach prevention.

Every adult is responsible for protecting the next generation of children. And we can't succeed in protecting them unless we establish a true zero-tolerance culture.

When he talked about the importance of the civil rights movement, Martin Luther King said that "History will have to record that the greatest tragedy of this period of social transition was not the strident clamor of the bad people, but the appalling silence of the good people."

That is still true today. For us to be silent on this issue is to fall short of our responsibilities as leaders of a battle to protect society's most innocent and most vulnerable, our children.

We must seed our communities with our knowledge and our passion. Remember that this communication starts with each other, the Project Safe Childhood partners. U.S. Attorneys' offices need to be calling their state and local partners constantly—and we at the Department should be hearing from you. I don't ever want to hear that one of our U.S. Attorneys didn't return your call. And I don't want to hear that an ICAC [Internet Crimes Against Children Task Force] commander didn't return a U.S. Attorney call.

When we work together, when we talk to each other, we save kids from unthinkable abuse—it's that simple.

In a recent District of Minnesota case, the importance of community involvement, communications and the strength of the Project Safe Childhood structure was evident when a tip from a concerned citizen led to the indictment of a registered sex offender on five counts of production of child pornography. The defendant was observed at a public park with a group of young boys and a digital camera. The concerned citizen called the St. Paul Police Department, who ultimately requested assistance from the Minnesota Internet Crimes Against Children Task Force, who then included the National Center for Missing and Exploited Children, the FBI, the U.S. Secret Service, Midwest Children's Resource Center, the Ramsey County Attorney's Office and the U.S. Attorney's Office in the investigation

With all hands on deck, it was discovered that the defendant had been manufacturing child pornography for years. The Project Safe Childhood coalition in Minnesota was ultimately able to rescue several boys from continuing abuse and exploitation

That my friends, is a true success story.

It reminds us that we can't communicate too much when it comes to investigating and prosecuting these crimes. We can't have too many partnerships or too much help from everyday citizens when it comes to protecting our kids.

That is why Project Safe Childhood exists, and that is the power of its potential.

But as I said earlier, even more is needed. We need to take this effort to the next level.

Make Sure All Adults Understand the Danger

We all need to be on the same page and we should be talking to parents, teachers and other community groups as often as we can. Keep learning from your partners, then keep sharing with your communities—teach them how to recognize trends and signs of abuse, end how to take action if they suspect that a child is being abused.

When responsible citizens [see] how determined pedophiles and predators are to get access to our children . . . they, like you, will be moved to help.

This message needs to be heard at the local Chamber of Commerce meeting as much as it does at the school board meeting. Because every adult is responsible for protecting the next generation of children. And we can't succeed in protecting them unless we establish a true zero-tolerance culture

I think the President put it very well when he signed the Adam Walsh Act. He said: "Protecting our children is our solemn responsibility. It's what we must do. When a child's life or innocence is taken it is a terrible loss—it's an act of unforgivable cruelty. Our society has a duty to protect our children from exploitation and danger."

As leaders, our duty is clear. We must not only arrest, investigate and prosecute—we must speak, and speak again, and speak more loudly and more clearly if we aren't being heard.

It's uncomfortable to describe the rape of a three-year-old. It's uncomfortable to hear about it.

But we must tell the stories, and we must make it okay to listen.

Because when responsible citizens stop and see what is being done to our kids . . . and how determined pedophiles and predators are to get access to children and continue committing these unthinkable crimes . . . they, like you, will be moved to help.

The average citizen will step between molesters and their victims.

They will notify authorities when they think something "just isn't right."

They will follow the example of Tracie Dean, whose story was shared by Oprah Winfrey earlier this year. Tracie took action when she couldn't stop thinking about the little girl she saw at a convenience store who "just didn't belong" with the man next to her.

Tracie couldn't put the child's face out of her head. Maybe it was the look in her eyes, she didn't know . . . but she returned to the convenience store—hundreds of miles from her home—and worked with the store manager and ultimately with local police to find out the story of the little girl she had seen, the girl she was so worried about and she didn't know quite why.

As it turns out, Tracie was right. The man who she'd seen with the child was arrested and has been charged with statutory rape, sexual abuse and sodomy in connection with that girl and a 17-year-old boy also found living with him. Doctors confirmed that the young girl had been severely sexually assaulted.

Thanks to Tracie, that little girl is finally safe from the man who was hurting her. She is now in foster care and we pray that her wounds—both physical and emotional—are healing today.

We have the infrastructure, we have the desire and we have the responsibility to create a nation of Tracie Deans.

We have the power to change the battlefield, and the victory of safe childhoods will be our legacy.

If everyone acts like she did, the number of people actively protecting children every day, everywhere they go, will absolutely dwarf the number of twisted souls who are trying to hurt them.

We have the power to change the battlefield, and the victory of safe childhoods will be our legacy.

We Are in a War Against Evil

People often ask me what keeps me up at night. Obviously the threat of a terrorist attack never leaves my mind, and it is the top priority of our government to keep that from happening.

But it is the faces of child victims that haunt my dreams. I can see their eyes, that awful emptiness, as if their tiny souls are trying to detach themselves from their desecrated bodies.

I see the victim's images as part of my work. But now they are part of my heart, and I am not going to tire in this fight to protect them.

I know you are with me. That is why, today, we are brothers and sisters in a common cause—you and me, standing shoulder to shoulder, like sentinels at the watch.

President Bush has talked to the American people about the need for armies of compassion to rise up to battle the evils of our society.

We are not yet there on this issue, but our band of soldiers grows stronger every day. Parents and community groups will be our infantry. The Internet Crimes Against Children Task Forces will be our cavalry. And our prosecutors will be our artillery.

The next time I see you all, I want our battalion ready to go. I look forward to meeting with you on that day when we are routinely catching and prosecuting the criminal who is buying child pornography and has signed up to be a summer camp counselor . . . but hasn't yet touched a child.

A day when justice is served before an already-abusive parent invites his daughter's friends over for a slumber party.

I want these pedophiles off the streets. I want them put away for as long as the law will allow.

A day when we never hear from the people who brag on the Internet about being revolutionaries, fighting for the so-called "sexual rights of children"—as though they are doing kids a favor by sexually molesting and exploiting them.

I want these pedophiles off the streets.

I want them put away for as long as the law will allow.

And I want society to act as one united front against this threat.

You and I won't tolerate the continued victimization, exploitation and desecration of our children.

And soon, with your help, no one else in this nation will, either.

May God bless and guide your important work, and may he continue to bless this great nation. Thank you.

Child Molestation Has Reached Epidemic Proportions

Dana D. Kelley

Dana D. Kelley is a contributing writer to the Arkansas Democrat-Gazette *and resides in Jonesboro, Arkansas.*

What are the odds that within a week two child molesters would storm random schools and kill children? Maybe much higher than you think.

Consider the similarities in the attacks in Bailey, Colo., and Nickel Mines, Pa. [which took place on September 29, 2006, and on October 2, 2006, respectively]. Both appeared to be well-planned and premeditated. Both schools were in rural communities. In each instance, the gunman wanted only young female hostages, letting boys and teachers go. Neither killer had any known connection to the school or the victims, and each committed suicide.

The second shooting mirrored the first so much that "copycat" questions arose immediately. And it's hard to imagine, given the incredible news coverage of the first shooting in Colorado, that the Pennsylvania killer hadn't at least heard about it. But there's a crucial concept to keep in mind related to such sweeping categorizations, because the word "copycat" implies an unnatural mimicking inspired by observation. A dog acting like a dog is not a copycat, for example. It's just being a dog.

Molestation Epidemic Is Downplayed

The larger question growing out of these recent murders relates to the nature and self-destructive ends of sexual perversion. The most significant commonality between the two incidents wasn't the methods, but the motive. Apparently both the drifter in Colorado and the milkman in Pennsylvania wanted to sexually molest young girls as a final act of life.

These two cases obviously represent extreme examples, but there is a child molestation epidemic at hand. It hasn't garnered the mass media coverage it should warrant, however, and politics has definitely played a role in the squelching.

The homosexual lobby vehemently objects anytime the overrepresentation of gays among child-preying sex offenders comes up. The teachers lobby is desperate to avoid any analysis of child molesters by profession that could result in a media hit job like that done on Catholic priests. Congress itself has seemed irresolute on the issue at times. . . .

But political correctness cannot be allowed to stand in the way of meeting this epidemic head on. Here's some disturbing information you may not know.

First of all, very few child molesters (less than 10 percent) are prosecuted. When caught, the first arrest almost never occurs on the molester's first crime. A National Institute of Mental Health study found, incredibly, that the average molester of females will victimize 50 girls before being caught and convicted. The average molester of boys is even worse, accumulating 150 victims before arrest and conviction.

The prolific practices of sexual predators create huge numbers of victims. About 1-in-3 girls will be sexually abused by age 18. Almost that many boys will be, too.

The National Center for Missing and Exploited Children reports that more than half of sexually abused children are victimized before they reach their seventh birthday, and 84 percent before age 12.

The Internet Has Created a New Threat

This epidemic is of recent vintage. It's mushroomed along with some enabling technology and trends, most notably the explosion of Internet pornography and personal Web sites. In the past decade, child pornography sites, which are illegal around the globe, have proliferated and now number more than 100,000.

As Attorney General Alberto Gonzales told Congress in September [2006,] the pictures and videos on those Internet sites aren't of the hotel room adult-channel variety. They are horrific, stomach-turning images—he described screaming toddlers brutally raped and sodomized by grown men—and each one documents an actual crime scene.

There are also 300 million Web pages containing legal porn, plus the countless new avenues that molesters have through chat rooms and the like to find children all over the country. It's a quaint twist of memory to recall that prior to 1994 only five states had sex offender registry programs. Today all 50 do, and like other epidemics, the sheer volume is overwhelming our resources.

No Second Chances for Molesters

To combat chronic child molesters, the first fact that must be faced is that someone who lusts after a 6-year-old child is not like you and me, not at all. Part of the reason we can't fathom someone walking into a school and shooting 10 young girls is because we also can't fathom wanting to have sex with them.

Some of the things being measured about violence in child molesters is shocking. The likelihood to commit murder is extraordinarily high among violent molesters with a criminal record. Even higher is the suicide rate among sex-offense-only molesters—200 times that of the general population. This information should aid us in preventing more child molester massacres. By the time we identify a child molester, he's almost always already victimized many children. If he has any felony convictions, the odds are that he's a killer (with suicidal tendencies) waiting to happen.

At that point, deterrence is no longer possible. The only hope is separation from prospective victims: identifying, catching and incarcerating molesters for life. This particular breed of predator is new, and we need new laws to protect our children—laws that can recognize the dangerous combination of factors that creates walking time-bomb molesters.

At the first display of violence, there can be no second chance for a child sex predator. Otherwise, statistics tell us that eventually there will be no chance at all for some innocent victim.

Research and Statistics Debunk Common Misconceptions

Association for the Treatment of Sexual Abusers

The Association for the Treatment of Sexual Abusers is an international, nonprofit organization incorporated in 1984 that supports effective management of sex offenders through alliances with law enforcement, mental health professionals, lawmakers, and community groups.

Sexual offending, like many mental and medical conditions, cannot be cured. Contemporary cognitive behavioral treatment, however, helps offenders learn to control their behavior. By recognizing and changing the thoughts that rationalize and justify sexually abusive behavior, sex offenders can become more aware of the harm caused to victims and view their own behavior differently. As well, sex offenders learn to identify their patterns of behavior, including the people, places, and things that put them at risk for offending. Through avoidance of certain situations, acquiring new coping skills, and learning to meet their emotional and sexual needs in healthy ways, motivated sex offenders can prevent future offending. Although some sex offenders may continue to be attracted to children, they can learn to avoid acting on their impulses. Consider this analogy: When adults get married, they do not stop being attracted to other people. They *do* stop acting on that attraction, because the way they think about the commitment of marriage helps them to control their behavior. Likewise, many chemically addicted persons continue to struggle with urges to use drugs or alcohol. Through treatment and recovery, however, they choose to change their behavior because they are committed to a new, healthy and productive lifestyle.

Early studies, conducted in the 70's and 80's, were unable to detect differences in recidivism [re-offense] rates between sex offenders who had undergone treatment and those who had not. This finding was widely publicized, leading to skepticism about the benefits of treatment, and opening the door to punitive public policies. Actually, although the research is not unequivocal, treatment has been found to decrease sex offense recidivism. Recent, statistically sophisticated studies with extremely large combined samples have found that contemporary cognitive-behavioral treatment does help to reduce rates of sexual reoffending by as much as 40%. However, treatment does not work equally well for all offenders (like any psychological or mental health treatment—or medical interventions, for that matter). Some research indicates that comprehensive programs and length of time in treatment are also important factors in the effectiveness of treatment. Treatment failure is associated with higher recidivism rates, and some research indicates that sex offenders who successfully complete a treatment program reoffend less often than those who do not demonstrate that they "got it."

Most Sex Offenders Don't Re-Offend

There is a perception that the vast majority of sex offenders will repeat their crimes. Research studies by the US Dept. of Justice and the Canadian Government have found, however, that sexual offense recidivism rates are much lower than commonly believed, averaging between 14 and 20% over 5-year follow-up periods. Studies that have tracked sex offenders over longer follow-up periods have found that pedophiles who molest boys, and rapists of adult women, were the types of offenders most likely to recidivate at rates of 52% and 39% respectively. Repeat offenders are more likely to reoffend than first-time offenders. Those who comply with probation and treatment have lower reoffense rates that those who violate the conditions of their release. Sex offenders who target strangers are more dangerous than those with victims inside their own family.

Although extensive media attention is paid to child abductions, such cases occur relatively rarely, and less than 1% of sex crimes involve murder.

It is also important to recognize that official recidivism statistics are always lower than actual reoffense rates, because some sex offenders commit many sex crimes that go unreported and undetected. It is estimated that less than 10% of all sex crimes result in a criminal conviction. This means that there are many sex offenders in our communities who have not yet been identified.

Although extensive media attention is paid to child abductions, such cases occur relatively rarely, and less than 1% of sex crimes involve murder. Despite myths of stranger danger, the vast majority of sexually abused children (80–90%) are molested by family members and close friends or acquaintances.

Risks Determined and Treatment Provided

Progress has been made in the science of risk assessment, which allows us to determine the likelihood that a sex offender will commit a new sex crime in the future. Although we cannot predict with certainty that any particular offender will act in a specific way, we can estimate, with moderate accuracy, whether or not an offender belongs to a high- or low-risk group. Using risk factors that have been correlated with recidivism, qualified practitioners can use scientific risk assessment tools to screen offenders into risk categories. These procedures are similar to the ways in which insurance companies assess risk and assign premiums, and how doctors evaluate a patient's risk for developing a medical illness. Risk assessment allows us to identify the most dangerous sex offenders, and apply the most intensive interventions to those who need the greatest level of supervision, treatment, and restriction.

Because treated offenders reoffend at lower rates than untreated offenders, providing therapeutic intervention saves money on investigation, prosecution, incarceration, and victim services.

Most states require convicted sex offenders to participate in treatment while in prison or on probation. According to the Safer Society Survey [conducted in 2003] there are 1,549 sex offender treatment programs in the U.S. Most of them are community-based (80%) with about 40% of them treating adults, and the rest targeting adolescents and children with sexual behavior problems. Although numbers vary widely, on average, about 70 adult sex offenders are treated each year in each outpatient program.

It is estimated that whereas treatment of sex offenders costs about $5,000 per year, incarceration costs more than $20,000 per year per offender. A [2003] study of the costs and benefits of treatment has found that treatment saves more money than it costs: about $4 is saved for every dollar spent on treatment services. The Preliminary Results from the Washington State Institute for Public Policy's Economic Analysis of Sex Offender Programs estimated that each taxpayer dollar spent on a cognitive-behavioral program for adult offenders returns between $1.19 and $5.27 in victim and taxpayers benefits. Because treated offenders reoffend at lower rates than untreated offenders, providing therapeutic intervention saves money on investigation, prosecution, incarceration, and victim services.

All Sex Offenders Are Not the Same

Although virtually all pedophiles are child molesters, not all child molesters are pedophiles. Pedophiles are men with a clear sexual preference for children rather than adults. Child molesters are described as individuals who have committed a sexual offense against a child victim. There are, however, no "pure" types, and offenders are best conceptualized as closer to one end of the continuum or the other.

Pedophiles

- True pedophiles are motivated by their sexual attraction to children and their offenses are directed toward vulnerable children whom they court or groom for the purpose of victimization.

- Offenders who seek out children to victimize by placing themselves in positions of trust, authority, and easy access to youngsters can have hundreds of victims over the course of their lifetimes. One study found that the average number of victims for non-incestuous pedophiles who molest girls is 20, for pedophiles who prefer boys, over 100.

- Predatory pedophiles, especially those who molest boys, are the sex offenders who have the highest recidivism rates. Over long follow-up periods, more than half of convicted pedophiles are rearrested for a new offense.

- Pedophiles frequently are uncomfortable with adult intimacy and may spend their lives maneuvering to be near children. They may be extremely charming and skilled at manipulating adults, and they will use adult relationships to gain access to children.

- The pedophile may spend years working his way up to a position of authority and trust within a church, school, or youth organization in order to have access to children.

- Their offenses are usually predatory—directed towards children whom they engage in relationships for the purpose of victimization. However, pedophiles may also sexually abuse children in their own families.

- Pedophiles are sometime referred to as "fixated," "preferential," "predatory," "extrafamilial," or "nonfamilial."

Non-pedophilic Child Molesters

- The non-predatory molester tends to be a man whose primary sexual attraction is toward adults, but who may molest children in a maladaptive attempt to meet emotional needs.

- Incest offenders are more likely to be non-pedophilic molesters.

- Research has found that many heterosexual incest offenders have sexual interests that are indistinguishable from those of normal males.

- However, there are many research studies that indicate, under conditions of anonymous survey guaranteed confidentiality, or polygraph, that approximately 60% of incest offenders also molest non-relative children.

- Data suggest that incestuous offenders, regardless of the gender of the victim, have lower numbers of victims and are less likely to be rearrested for new sex crimes after they've been convicted.

- Non-pedophilic molesters may turn to a child for sex out of a perceived inability to be close with an adult partner, out of poor self-esteem, or to escape feelings of powerlessness and loneliness.

- This type of offender often has appropriate (but dysfunctional) relationships with peers and may be married.

- These child molesters are sometimes called "regressed," "situational," or "opportunistic," and often are apprehended in incestuous situations.

- Outcome studies have demonstrated consistently low rates of recidivism for incestuous offenders. However, it is important to note that incest victims are among the least likely to report sexual crimes, and incest is one of the most damaging types of sexual abuse to victims.

- Intrafamilial offenders may be among those most likely to benefit from therapeutic intervention.

What Is a Sexual Predator?

The definition of "predator" differs from state to state, but is generally reserved for the most dangerous sex offenders. Many states use nearly identical words to describe this type of sex offender and the offenses he perpetrates. In the words of the Kansas Sexually Violent Predator Act, "predatory acts" are those *"acts directed towards strangers or individuals with whom relationships have been established or promoted for the primary purpose of victimization."* The state of California states: *"'Predatory' means an act is directed toward a stranger, a person of casual acquaintance with whom no substantial relationship exists, or an individual with whom a relationship has been established or promoted for the primary purpose of victimization."* In some states, the definition includes criteria involving the use of violence, weapons, or causing injury during the commission of a sex crime, or those offenders who have had multiple victims. Repeat offenders, and those who have committed abduction of children or adults for sexual purposes may also be considered predators.

There is no evidence that community notification reduces sex offense recidivism or increases community safety.

It is important to remember that although recent media attention has been focused on child abduction and molestation, rapists of adult women can also be highly dangerous sexual predators. They often have many victims, and are more likely than child molesters to use violence or weapons to gain compliance from victims. The majority of victims of sexually motivated murders are adult women.

Community Notification Is Ineffective

In 1994, following the 1989 abduction of an 11 year old boy in Minnesota, a federal law was passed mandating sex offenders to register with local law enforcement agencies so that their current whereabouts are known ("Jacob Wetterling Crimes Against Children and Sexually Violent Offender Registration Act," 1994). In 1996, President Clinton signed "Megan's Law," which requires states to disseminate information to the public about sex offenders who live in close proximity.

About half of the states in the U.S. assign offenders to one of three risk levels and notify the public differentially according to the offender's risk. Other states employ broad community notification, publicizing the location of all sex offenders without regard for risk assessment.

There is no evidence that community notification reduces sex offense recidivism or increases community safety. The only study to date found no statistically significant difference in recidivism rates between offenders who were subjected to notification in Washington (19% recidivism) and those who were not (22% recidivism). Sex offenders who were subjected to community notification were, however, arrested more quickly for new sex crimes than those not publicly identified. It was found that 63% of the new sex offenses occurred in the jurisdiction where notification took place, suggesting that notification did not deter offenders or motivate them to venture outside their jurisdictions (where they would be less likely identified) to commit crimes. Based on these findings, the authors concluded that community notification appeared to have little effect on sex offense recidivism.

Interestingly, most results have indicated that citizens report increased anxiety due to notification because of the lack of strategies offered for protecting themselves from sex offenders.

Research suggests that about one-third to one-half of sex offenders subjected to community notification experience dire events such as the loss of a job or home, threats or harassment, or property damage. Physical assault seems to occur in 5–16% of cases. About 19% of sex offenders report that these negative consequences have affected other members of their households.

There is no research to support the idea that residence restrictions prevent repeat sex crimes.

It has been suggested that notification may, ironically, interfere with its stated goal of enhancing public safety by exacerbating the stressors (e.g., isolation, disempowerment, shame, depression, anxiety, lack of social supports) that may trigger some sex offenders to relapse. Such dynamic factors have been associated with increased recidivism, and although sex offenders inspire little sympathy from the public, ostracizing them may inadvertently increase their risk.

Residency Restrictions Are Not Helpful

Fourteen states (Alabama, Arkansas, California, Florida, Georgia, Illinois, Indiana, Iowa, Kentucky, Louisiana, Ohio, Oklahoma, Oregon, and Tennessee) have enacted buffer zones which prohibit sex offenders from residing within close proximity to a school, park, day care center, or school bus stop. The least restrictive distance requirement is in Illinois (500 feet), but most common are 1,000 to 2,000 foot boundaries.

There is no research to support the idea that residence restrictions prevent repeat sex crimes.

In Colorado it was found that molesters who reoffended while on probation were randomly scattered throughout the geographical area, and did not seem to live closer than non-recidivists to schools or child care centers.

In Minnesota, sex offenders' proximity to schools or parks was not a factor in recidivism, nor did it impact community safety. In fact, the opposite was found to be true—a sex offender was more likely to travel to another neighborhood in which he could seek victims without being recognized.

Public safety and child protection are understandably the primary considerations when sex offender restrictions are imposed. Advocates of residence restrictions believe that such laws will diminish the likelihood that sex offenders will come in contact with children whom they might potentially victimize. However, concerns have been raised that such mandates might exacerbate the shortage of housing options for sex offenders and force them to move to rural areas where they would be increasingly isolated with few employment and treatment options (Minnesota Department of Corrections, 2003). The dispersal of parks and schools may lead to overlapping restriction zones, making it essentially impossible for sex offenders in some cities to find suitable housing. In some urban areas, offenders might be forced to cluster in high-crime neighborhoods. Such restrictions can lead to homelessness and transience, which interfere with effective tracking, monitoring, and close probationary supervision.

A survey of 135 sex offenders in Florida revealed that housing restrictions increased isolation, created financial and emotional stress, and led to decreased stability for sex offenders. Respondents also indicated that they did not perceive residence restrictions as helpful in risk management, and in fact, reported that such restrictions may inadvertently increase triggers for reoffense.

Set Policy Based on Facts, Not Fear

Public policy should be used to strengthen, not replace, other efforts designed to prevent sexual abuse. Sex offenders should be held responsible for their actions while receiving treatment to help them change their behavior. According to the Center for Sex Offender Management (operated under a grant from the U.S. Department of Justice), prevention of sexual violence requires a well-planned, comprehensive, inter-disciplinary response that begins with developing clear goals and objectives, implementing strategies based on empirical research, and collecting and analyzing data on an ongoing basis. Emotionally charged reactions to sex crimes often lead to legislation that is not driven by data or science but rather by outrage and fear. Lawmakers and citizens should advocate for research-based social policies that protect women and children as well as rehabilitate perpetrators. Policymakers should advocate for the most efficient and cost-effective implementation of laws based on the limited empirical research that exists.

1. Some sex offenders are highly dangerous and require more intensive interventions.

2. Community notification and residence restrictions should employ evidence based risk assessment procedures and differential strategies concordant with the level of threat that an offender poses to a community.

3. Collaborative efforts should exist between citizens, law enforcement, offenders, and treatment providers to render management, probationary supervision, and rehabilitation services that promote community safety.

4. Educational efforts should be directed at the prevention of sexual abuse. Communities are entitled to factual and research-based information and education about sexual violence and sexual perpetrators.

5. Empirical inquiry is needed into the impact and effectiveness of public policies designed to prevent sexual violence. Funding for research investigating the impact and effectiveness of sexual violence policies should be a priority.

Americans Exaggerate Threats Posed by Sexual Predators

Benjamin Radford

Benjamin Radford is the author of Media Mythmakers: How Journalists, Activists, and Advertisers Mislead Us. *He is the managing editor of* The Skeptical Inquirer: The Magazine for Science and Reason, *in which the following article appeared.*

"Protect the children." Over the years that mantra has been applied to countless real and perceived threats. America has scrambled to protect its children from a wide variety of dangers including school shooters, cyberbullying, violent video games, snipers, Satanic Ritual Abuse, pornography, the Internet, and drugs.

Hundreds of millions of taxpayer dollars have been spent protecting children from one threat or other, often with little concern for how expensive or effective the remedies are—or how serious the threat actually is in the first place. So it is with America's latest panic: sexual predators.

According to lawmakers and near-daily news reports, sexual predators lurk everywhere: in parks, at schools, in the malls—even in children's bedrooms, through the Internet. A few rare (but high-profile) incidents have spawned an unprecedented deluge of new laws enacted in response to the public's fear. Every state has notification laws to alert communities about former sex offenders. Many states have banned sex offenders from living in certain areas, and are tracking them using satellite technology. Other states have gone even further; state emergency leaders in Florida and Texas, for example, are developing plans to route convicted sex offenders away from public emergency shelters during hurricanes. "We don't want

Benjamin Radford, "Predator Panic: A Closer Look," *The Skeptical Inquirer*, vol. 30, no. 5, September 2006, pp. 20–21, 69. Copyright © 2006 Committee for the Scientific Investigation of Claims of the Paranormal. Reproduced by permission.

them in the same shelters as others," said Texas Homeland Security Director Steve McCraw. (How exactly thousands of desperate and homeless storm victims are to be identified, screened, and routed in an emergency is unclear.)

An Epidemic?

To many people, sex offenders pose a serious and growing threat—especially on the Internet. [Former] Attorney General Alberto Gonzales has made them a top priority this year, launching raids and arrest sweeps. According to Senate Majority Leader Bill Frist, "the danger to teens is high." On the April 18, 2005, *CBS Evening News* broadcast, correspondent Jim Acosta reported that "when a child is missing, chances are good it was a convicted sex offender." (Acosta is incorrect: If a child goes missing, a convicted sex offender is among the least likely explanations, far behind runaways, family abductions, and the child being lost or injured.) On his NBC series "To Catch a Predator," *Dateline* reporter Chris Hansen claimed that "the scope of the problem is immense," and "seems to be getting worse." Hansen claimed that Web predators are "a national epidemic," while Alberto Gonzales stated that there are 50,000 potential child predators online.

The reality is that very few sex offenders commit further sex crimes.

Sex offenders are clearly a real threat, and commit horrific crimes. Those who prey on children are dangerous, but how common are they? How great is the danger? After all, there are many dangers in the world—from lightning to Mad Cow Disease to school shootings—that are genuine but very remote. Let's examine some widely repeated claims about the threat posed by sex offenders.

One in Five?

According to a May 3, 2006, ABC News report, "One in five children is now approached by online predators." This alarming statistic is commonly cited in news stories about prevalence of Internet predators, but the factoid is simply wrong. The "one in five statistic" can be traced back to a 2001 Department of Justice study issued by the National Center for Missing and Exploited Children ("The Youth Internet Safety Survey") that asked 1,501 American teens between 10 and 17 about their online experiences. Anyone bothering to actually read the report will find a very different picture. Among the study's conclusions: "Almost one in five (19 percent) . . . received an unwanted sexual solicitation in the past year." (A "sexual solicitation" is defined as a "request to engage in sexual activities or sexual talk or give personal sexual information that were unwanted or, whether wanted or not, made by an adult." Using this definition, one teen asking another teen if her or she is a virgin—or got lucky with a recent date—could be considered "sexual solicitation.") Not a single one of the reported solicitations led to any actual sexual contact or assault. Furthermore, almost half of the "sexual solicitations" came not from "predators" or adults but from other teens—in many cases the equivalent of teen flirting. When the study examined the type of Internet "solicitation" parents are most concerned about (e.g., someone who asked to meet the teen somewhere, called the teen on the telephone, or sent gifts), the number drops from "one in five" to just 3 percent.

This is a far cry from an epidemic of children being "approached by online predators." As the study noted, "The problem highlighted in this survey is not just adult males trolling for sex. Much of the offending behavior comes from other youth [and] from females." Furthermore, "Most young people seem to know what to do to deflect these sexual 'come ons.'" The reality is far less grave than the ubiquitous "one in five" statistic suggests.

Most Offenders Do Not Repeat

Much of the concern over sex offenders stems from the perception that if they have committed one sex offense, they are almost certain to commit more. This is the reason given for why sex offenders (instead of, say, murderers or armed robbers) should be monitored and separated from the public once released from prison. While it's true that serial sex offenders (like serial killers) are by definition likely to strike again, the reality is that very few sex offenders commit further sex crimes.

The high recidivism rate among sex offenders is repeated so often that it is accepted as truth, but in fact recent studies show that the recidivism rates for sex offenses is not unusually high. According to a U.S. Bureau of Justice Statistics study ("Recidivism of Sex Offenders Released from Prison in 1994"), just five percent of sex offenders followed for three years after their release from prison in 1994 were arrested for another sex crime. A study released in 2003 by the Bureau of Justice Statistics found that within three years, 3.3 percent of the released child molesters were arrested again for committing another sex crime against a child. Three to five percent is hardly a high repeat offender rate.

While the abduction, rape, and killing of children by strangers is very, very rare, such incidents receive a lot of media coverage.

In the largest and most comprehensive study ever done of prison recidivism, the Justice Department found that sex offenders were in fact *less* likely to reoffend than other criminals. The 2003 study of nearly 10,000 men convicted of rape, sexual assault, and child molestation found that sex offenders had a re-arrest rate 25 percent lower than for all other criminals. Part of the reason is that serial sex offenders—those who pose the greatest threat—rarely get released from prison, and the ones who do are unlikely to re-offend. If released sex offenders are in fact no more likely to re-offend than murderers or armed robbers, there seems little justification for the public's fear and the monitoring laws targeting them. (Studies also suggest that sex offenders living near schools or playgrounds are no more likely to commit a sex crime than those living elsewhere.)

While the abduction, rape, and killing of children by strangers is very, very rare, such incidents receive a lot of media coverage, leading the public to overestimate how common these cases are.

News Media Fuels Hysteria

There are several reasons for the hysteria and fear surrounding sexual predators. The predator panic is largely fueled by the news media. News stories emphasize the dangers of Internet predators, convicted sex offenders, pedophiles, and child abductions. The *Today Show*, for example, ran a series of misleading and poorly designed hidden camera "tests" to see if strangers would help a child being abducted. *Dateline NBC* teamed up with a group called Perverted Justice to lure potential online predators to a house with hidden cameras. The program's ratings were so high that it spawned six follow-up "To Catch a Predator" specials. While the many men captured on film supposedly showing up to meet teens for sex is disturbing, questions have been raised about Perverted Justice's methods and accuracy. (For example, the predators are often found in unmoderated chatrooms frequented by those looking for casual sex—hardly places where most children spend their time.) Nor is it surprising that out of over a hundred million Internet users, a fraction of a percentage might be caught in such a sting.

Because there is little hard data on how widespread the problem of Internet predators is, journalists often resort to sensationalism, cobbling a few anecdotes and interviews together into a trend while glossing over data suggesting that the problem may not be as widespread as they claim. But good journalism requires that personal stories—no matter how emotional and compelling—must be balanced with facts and context. Much of the news coverage about sexual predation is not so much wrong as incomplete, lacking perspective.

Moral Panics

The news media's tendency toward alarmism only partly explains the concern. America is in the grip of a moral panic over sexual predators, and has been for many months. A *moral panic* is a sociological term describing a social reaction to a false or exaggerated threat to social values by moral deviants.

In a discussion of moral panics, sociologist Robert Bartholomew points out that a defining characteristic of the panics is that the "concern about the threat posed by moral deviants and their numerical abundance is far greater than can be objectively verified, despite unsubstantiated claims to the contrary." Furthermore, according to [Ehrich Goode and Nachman Ben-Yehuda in their 1994 book, *Moral Panics: The Social Construction of Deviance*] during a moral panic "most of the figures cited by moral panic 'claims-makers' are wildly exaggerated."

Misleading news stories influence lawmakers, who in turn react with genuine (and voter-friendly) moral outrage.

Indeed, we see exactly this trend in the panic over sexual predators. News stories invariably exaggerate the true extent of sexual predation on the Internet; the magnitude of the danger to children, and the likelihood that sexual predators will strike. (As it turns out, Attorney General Gonzales had taken his 50,000 Web predator statistic not from any government study or report, but from NBC's *Dateline* TV show. *Dateline*, in turn, had broadcast the number several times without checking its accuracy. In an interview on NPR's *On the Media* program, Hansen admitted that he had no source for the statistic, and stated that "It was attributed to, you know, law enforcement, as an estimate, and it was talked about as sort of an extrapolated number.") According to *Wall Street Journal* writer Carl Bialik, journalists "often will use dubious numbers to advance that goal [of protecting children] . . . one of the reasons that this is allowed to happen is that there isn't really a natural critic. . . . Nobody really wants to go on the record saying, 'It turns out this really isn't a big problem.'"

Panicky Laws

Besides needlessly scaring children and the public, there is a danger to this quasi-fabricated, scare-of-the-week reportage: misleading news stories influence lawmakers, who in turn react with genuine (and voter-friendly) moral outrage. Because nearly any measure intended (or claimed) to protect children will be popular and largely unopposed, politicians trip over themselves in the rush to endorse new laws that "protect the children."

Politicians, child advocates, and journalists denounce current sex offender laws as ineffective and flawed, yet are rarely able to articulate exactly why new laws are needed. Instead, they cite each news story about a kidnapped child or Web predator as proof that more laws are needed, as if sex crimes would cease if only the penalties were harsher, or enough people were monitored. Yet the fact that rare crimes continue to be committed does not necessarily imply that current laws against those crimes are inadequate. By that standard, any law is ineffective if someone violates that law. We don't assume that existing laws against murder are ineffective simply because murders continue to be committed.

In July 2006, teen abduction victim Elizabeth Smart and child advocate John Walsh (whose murdered son Adam spawned *America's Most Wanted*) were instrumental in helping pass the most extensive national sex offender bill in history. According to Senator Orrin Hatch (R[epublican]-Utah), the bill's sponsor, Smart's 2002 "abduction by a convicted sex offender" might have been prevented had his bill been law. "I don't want to see others go through what I had to go through," said Smart. "This bill should go through without a thought." Yet bills passed without thought rarely make good laws. In fact, a closer look at the cases of Elizabeth Smart and Adam Walsh demonstrate why sex offender registries *do not* protect children. Like most people who abduct children, Smart's kidnapper, Brian David Mitchell, was not a convicted sex offender. Nor was Adam Walsh abducted by a sex offender. Apparently unable to find a vocal advocate for a child who had actually been abducted by a convicted sex offender, Hatch used Smart and Walsh to promote an agenda that had nothing to do with the circumstances of their abductions. The two high-profile abductions (neither by sex offenders) were somehow claimed to demonstrate the urgent need for tighter restrictions on sex offenders. Hatch's bill, signed by President Bush on July 27, will likely have little effect in protecting America's children.

Simply knowing where a released sex offender lives—or is at any given moment—does not ensure that he or she won't be near potential victims.

The last high-profile government effort to prevent Internet predation occurred in December 2002, when President Bush signed the Dot-Kids Implementation and Efficiency Act into law, creating a special safe Internet "neighborhood" for children. Elliot Noss, president of Internet address registrar Tucows Inc., correctly predicted that the domain had "absolutely zero" chance of being effective. The ".kids.us" domain is now a largely ignored Internet footnote that has done little or nothing to protect children.

Tragic Misdirection

The issue is not whether children need to be protected; of course they do. The issues are whether the danger to them is great, and whether the measures proposed will ensure their safety. While some efforts—such as longer sentences for repeat offenders—are well-reasoned and likely to be effective, those focused on separating sex offenders from the public are of little value because they are based on a faulty premise. Simply knowing where a released sex offender lives—or is at any given moment—does not ensure that he or she won't be near potential victims. Since relatively few sexual assaults are committed by released sex offenders, the concern over the danger is wildly disproportionate to the real threat. Efforts to protect children are well-intentioned, but legislation should be based on facts and reasoned argument instead of fear in the midst of a national moral panic.

The tragic irony is that the panic over sex offenders distracts the public from the real danger, a far greater threat to children than sexual predators: parental abuse and neglect. The vast majority of crimes against children are committed not by released sex offenders but instead by the victim's own family, church clergy, and family friends. According to a 2003 report by the Department of Human Services, hundreds of thousands of children are abused and neglected each year by their parents and caregivers, and more than 1,500 American children died from that abuse in 2003—most of the victims under four years old. That is more than *four children killed per day*—not by convicted sexual offenders or Internet predators, but by those entrusted to care for them. According to the National Center for Missing and Exploited Children, "danger to children is greater from someone they or their family knows than from a stranger."

If journalists, child advocates, and lawmakers are serious about wanting to protect children, they should turn from the burning matchbook in front of them to face the blazing forest fire behind them. The resources allocated to tracking ex-felons who are unlikely to reoffend could be much more effectively spent on preventing child abuse in the home and hiring more social workers.

Eventually this predator panic will subside and some new threat will take its place. Expensive, ineffective, and unworkable laws will be left in its wake when the panic passes. And no one is protecting America from that.

Clarifying the Facts Can Strengthen Public Policy

Eric Lotke and Herbert J. Hoelter

Eric Lotke is an attorney, has served as a professor of law, and is the director of policy and research at the Justice Policy Institute. Herbert J. Hoelter is the cofounder, with Dr. Jerome G. Miller, or the National Center on Institutions and Alternatives, Inc.; he is considered a leading expert on the United States criminal justice system and policies.

Few offenses evoke more fear and loathing than sexual offenses. The idea stirs up images of innocent children deceived and victimized by scheming predators. Neighborhoods, fueled by sexual registries, are concerned, and intent on finding ways to reduce the frequency and severity of this personally destructive crime.

This review is intended to summarize basic facts about sex offenses and sexual offending. The goal is to clarify current knowledge and focus attention on the policies most likely to reduce the incidence and increase safety in communities. This report highlights the salient facts and discusses how they apply to public policy, so future policy can be crafted to improve safety and reduce future sexual victimization.

Families

Most sexual victimization takes place within families and among friends. Even though parents warn children about strangers, the vast majority of sexual offenses occur among people who are known and trusted—parents, siblings, friends, teachers, coaches or anyone within the family's "zone of association."

- Victimization of juveniles usually takes place within families (34%) and among friends (59%). Juveniles are rarely victimized by strangers (7%).

- Victimization of adults generally occurs among acquaintances (61%) and family members (12%). Victimization by strangers is far less common (27%).

- Nearly half (44%) of men imprisoned for a sex crime victimized their own child, stepchild or other family member. Rarely (7%) was the victim a stranger.

- The vast majority (84%) of sexual assaults on children below age 12 occur in a residence.

Policy Implications

- *Knowledge*: The people who need to know the most about the offense learn about it as soon as it is revealed. They do not need web pages, public registries or satellite tracking to tell them about the location of the perpetrator. They already know it.

- *Protection*: Children in private places are at greater risk. Children in public places such as school yards and playgrounds are protected by their visibility and their peers, so distance limits (e.g., not within 2,000 feet of a playground) are superfluous.

- *Victim Privacy*: Notifying the public about the identity of the perpetrator also often identities the victim. Public shaming of an incest offender is humiliating to the victim and the rest of the family.

Low Rate of Repeat Offenders

There is a widespread misperception that people who commit sexual crimes do it again and again. The research, however, directly contradicts this. Recidivism rates for sex offenses are relatively low, typically running in the 3–13% range, and among the lowest of all types of crimes.

Some notification schemes can actually increase the risk of reoffense.

The largest, most sophisticated analysis was performed by Karl Hanson, Solicitor General of Canada. His 2004 quantitative meta-analysis examined research evidence and recidivism risk factors in a total of 95 studies involving 31,000 sexual offenders with an average follow-up time of 5 years. Hanson's findings include:

- Overall recidivism rate for new sex crimes: 13.7%

- Recidivism rate for child molestation: 12.7%

- Recidivism rate for child molestation within families: 8.4%

- Recidivism rate for rape: 18.9%

A less nuanced study of former prisoners performed by the U.S. Bureau of Justice Statistics (BJS) reached similar conclusions, and found that people convicted of sex crimes had much lower reoffense rates than people convicted of other crimes. The BJS study followed 9,700 people incarcerated for sex crimes for three years after release. The findings include:

- 5.3% of people imprisoned for sex crimes were rearrested for another sex crime.

- 3.3% of people imprisoned for child molestation were rearrested for another sex crime against a child.

In contrast, the general rearrest rate for people released from prison was 68%. The highest rates were stealing motor vehicles (79%) and possessing or selling stolen property (77%).

The myth of high reoffense rates for sexual offenders is supported by some facts that are easily misinterpreted or misunderstood:

- Many individuals commit multiple offenses prior to being caught, often in pattern with the same victims over a long course of time. Thus, repeat numbers can be quite high—but it is important to distinguish repeats "before caught" from repeats "once caught." In most cases, the first known offense is also the last—though there may have been multiple priors.

- The risk of sexual recidivism is lower than the risk of recidivism of most other crimes. However, the risk that any *particular* individual will commit a sex crime is greater among people who have previously committed a sex crime than among other people. Thus, the U.S. Bureau of Justice Statistics can truthfully report that "sex offenders were about four times more likely than non-sex offenders to be arrested for another sex crime"—even though the study's reoffense rate for sex crimes was just 5.3%.

- Studies offer a range of factual findings with wide ranges of heterogeneous types of crime. Statistically outlying studies of crimes with higher recidivism rates are often used to exemplify the entire class of sex offenses. Researchers may talk about recidivism rates "as low as" 3% or "up to" 40%, but the "up to" is often dropped out of reporting, leaving people with the impression that the higher figure is the whole truth.

- The chance that a person convicted of a sex crime will someday commit some other crime greatly exceeds the chance that he or she will commit another sex crime. The second offense may be possession of marijuana, driving drunk or shoplifting—but it increases the reoffense rate. Such subsequent misconduct carries its own concerns, but it is not the repeat incurable pedophile of myth. Indeed reoffense rates for all crimes among sex offenders is still lower than reoffense rates for all crimes among non-sex offenders. For example, the U.S. Bureau of Justice Statistics found:

- Child molester rearrest rate for new sex crime against a child: 3.3%

- All sex offender rearrest rate for new sex crime against a child: 2.2%

- All sex offenders rearrest rate for *any kind* of offense: 43%

- All offenders rearrest rate for *any kind* of offense: 68%

A necessary caution: all studies of recidivism are limited by the observer's knowledge. What isn't known can't be measured, so reoffense rates may be higher than instances captured by researchers. On the other hand, some subsequent allegations may be unfounded but they will still result in people being caught in "rearrest" figures.

Policy Implications

- *Overbreadth*: Most people who commit sex crimes will not commit another sexual offense after they are caught. Adding more people to the databases just hides the needle deeper in the haystack. Safety may be better served with smaller numbers of higher risk individuals in the database, rather than so many people listed in every community that resources are wasted and warnings becomes meaningless.

Predictability

Predicting the future is always risky, but Karl Hanson's database of 31,000 sexual offenders and nearly 2,000 recidivism predictions leads to some highly reliable statistical guidance about likelihood of reoffense.

- Actuarial instruments based on routine information (e.g., demographic and criminal history) have shown a high degree of predictive accuracy.

- Troubled childhood environments and prior sexual victimization are associated with sexual misconduct, though not significantly associated with recurrence after the first episode.

- Many commonly emphasized legal or clinical characteristics are not significantly related to sexual recidivism: lack of victim empathy, minimization of the seriousness of the offense, lack of motivation for treatment. In explanation, Hanson notes the difficulty of measuring remorse in criminal justice settings. Although psychotherapists often consider disclosure desirable and courts are lenient towards people who show remorse, "few of us, however, are inclined to completely reveal our faults and transgressions. . . . Offenders who minimize their crimes are at least indicating that sexual offending is wrong."

- Accurate indicators of sexual recidivism included measures of deviant sexual interest, antisocial orientation, lifestyle instability, impulse control and various personality disorders.

Policy Implications

- *Risk Assessment Instruments*: Many routine decisions in the justice system such as sentencing and parole use actuarial risk assessment instruments. Decisions regarding notification and civil commitment should use similar instruments, probably in conjunction with clinical observation. It follows that higher scores would lead towards increased supervision and intervention, and a wiser investment of justice resources.

- *Added Instability*: Lifestyle instability is a risk factor for reoffending, and social normalization reduces the risk. Yet interventions such as web based notification, community leafleting, burdensome regulations, public stigma and possible harassment and flight make it difficult to stabilize one's life. Thus, some notification schemes can actually increase the risk of reoffense.

- *Responsibility*: People who commit sex crimes must take full responsibility for their actions. Comprehensive treatment and community reintegration are excellent means of increasing personal responsibility and internal control, while notification is an external means of surveillance. Notification shifts responsibility to the community, which can undermine offenders' personal sense of responsibility and leave the impression they can do whatever they can get away with.

Treatment

Although there is a great deal of skepticism, and research is not yet conclusive, there is considerable and growing evidence that deviant sexual behavior can be reformed by treatment. Available research indicates that quality treatment can reduce recidivism by more than one-third.

- Margaret Alexander's 1999 meta-analysis of nearly 11,000 sex offenders from 79 separate studies found that people who participated in treatment programs had a combined rearrest rate of 7.2% compared to 17.6% among untreated individuals (a reduction of 59%).

- Karl Hanson's 2000 comprehensive meta-analysis found 10% of treatment subjects reoffended, compared to 17% of untreated subjects (a reduction of 41%).

- The Campbell Collaboration meta-analysis of 69 studies of 22,000 individuals found that treatment reduced recidivism by 37%.

- Gordon Hall's 1995 meta-analysis found that treatment reduced recidivism by 30%.

There is no downside to treatment and growing evidence that treatment reduces the risk of reoffense. It follows that treatment should be extensive and ongoing.

Most Sex Offenders
Are Not Murderers

Lisa L. Sample

Lisa L. Sample is an assistant professor at the School of Criminology and Criminal Justice at the University of Nebraska at Omaha.

On observation, it is clear that most of the current sex offender policies we have today, and those being proposed for the future, are the result of sexually related homicides against children committed by previously convicted sex offenders. For example, Megan Kanka, Jacob Wetterling, and Jessica Lunsford were all children who were abducted, sexually assaulted, and killed by repeat sex offenders, and all share the distinction of having sex offender legislation passed in their names. At the national level, in 1994, the Jacob Wetterling Crimes Against Children and Sexually Violent Offender Registration Act mandated that 10% of a state's funding under the Edward Bryne Memorial State and Local Law Enforcement Assistance grant program be used for establishing a statewide system for registering and tracking convicted sex offenders. The Wetterling Act was amended by the passage of "Megan's Law" in 1996, which requires states to make sex offender registry information available to the public. More recently, at the state level, Florida legislators passed the Jessica Lunsford Act, which lengthens the sentences that sex offenders will serve on conviction and requires lifetime tracking by global positioning satellite once sex offenders emerge from prison. The march of sex offender legislation is unlikely to stop here, however, as new cases of sexually motivated homicides against children occur.

Lisa L. Sample, "An Examination of the Degree to Which Sex Offenders Kill," *Criminal Justice Review*, vol.31, no. 3, September 2006, pp. 230–50. Copyright © 2006 by Georgia State University Research Foundation, Inc. Reproduced by permission of Sage Publications, Inc.

In May 2005, Shasta Groene, 8, and her brother Dylan, 9, were found missing from their Idaho home where the bodies of their mother, 13-year-old brother, and their mother's boyfriend were discovered. By July, Shasta had been found alive and in the custody of a previously convicted and registered sex offender, Joseph Duncan. She reported that she and her brother had been repeatedly sexually molested. Her brother Dylan was later found dead. The father of these children has now added his voice to the calls of Jessica Lunsford's and Polly Klass's fathers for Congress to enact additional sex offender legislation, a national sex offender registry. The hope is that this legislation would help prevent sex offenders from moving from state to state unnoticed. Although Congress has not moved to enact this legislation to date, it seems likely that it will pass in the future. The passage of a national registry would simply provide further evidence that current sex offender laws are predicated on sexually related homicides against children.

The media attention given to the murder of children by previously convicted sex offenders, and the subsequent passage of sex offender laws, has firmly established a connection between sex offending and homicide, at least for those offenders who offend against children. In many cases, however, these laws have not been applied to only sex offenders with child victims. In some states, notification has been applied to all sex offenders equally, irrespective of their crime type or age of their victims. Given the broad application of some sex offender policies, one implicit assumption then emerges: Many, if not most, sex offenders go on to kill. This assumption leads to two important questions, both of which have policy implications for the future. First, to what degree do sex offenses precede, or occur in conjunction with, a homicide? Second, are sex offenders more prone to committing homicide than other groups of offender types? Answers to these questions provide insight into the degree to which sex offender policies will help prevent lethal violence and may also help narrow the scope of our current laws so they may better address those that present the most danger to society.

This study explores simply one assumption underlying sex offender laws, the notion that sex offenders often kill their victims. Specifically, criminal history information from Illinois from 1990 to 1997 was analyzed to determine to what degree sex offenders are charged with murder in conjunction with their arrest for a sex crime and the likelihood of arrested sex offenders experiencing a future arrest for homicide. The results from this research are discussed in terms of the potential efficacy of current, and proposed, sex offender policies.

Faulty Assumptions

Undoubtedly, there are many assumptions about sex offenders and their behaviors that underlie sex offender laws. Inherent in laws requiring registration and global tracking of sex offenders is the notion that these offenders will inevitably reoffend. Why else would they be required to provide their addresses to the public and law enforcement agencies or have all their movements tracked and monitored? Also inherent in current sex offender policies is the assumption that sex offenders are a homogenous group of criminals, experiencing similar levels of reoffending. Why else would registration and community notification laws be applied to all sex offenders in some states regardless of their offense type, personal circumstance, or age of their victims? These are important assumptions to investigate, as they undeniably have implications for the success of sex offender polices at achieving goals of deterrence and prevention. What appears to have driven most of our current policies, however, is the sexual assault and murder of children. In fact, one has to wonder if Congress would have passed the Wetterling Act or "Megan's Law" if these children would have been abducted and raped but not killed. In this sense, the notion that sex offending and homicide are intricately intertwined appears to be at the root of our current legislation and is thus the subject of this research.

Few [sex offenders] murder their victims when committing a sexual assault, and rarely do sex offenders commit homicide in the future.

This investigation is not meant to dismiss the threat of sexually violent crime, particularly against children, or minimize the threat of lethal violence that may be associated with sex offenses. Nor is this study meant to diminish the pain the parents of murdered children feel or explain why these travesties have occurred. Rather, this examination is simply meant to highlight one assumption underlying current, and proposed, sex offender laws and assess that assumption against empirical evidence. This information will help demonstrate the consequences of enacting legislation based on passion rather than on empirical realities. . . .

Sex Crimes and Homicide

Given that most homicides come to the attention of the police and that homicide is the crime that is most often "cleared" by an arrest, these data should fairly accurately reflect the probability of sex offenders committing acts of murder. Rarely do homicide charges occur in conjunction with a sex crime, and seldom are sex offenders subsequently arrested for a homicide. If sex crimes "cluster," or occur in conjunction, with other behaviors, they more often include nonsexual assaults, kidnapping, and burglary than acts of murder. Robbery arrests more frequently included additional charges for homicide, and a greater proportion of persons in the robbery category were subsequently charged with a murder than sex offenders. To this end, "robbed and killed" more accurately reflects the clustering of criminal behaviors in Illinois than "raped and killed." However, no crime type appears to precede or occur in conjunction with homicide with great frequency.

In addition, specific sex offense charges seldom occur in conjunction with other non-sexual crimes. Only about one quarter of arrests that involved a sex offense charge in 1990 had additional charges for other crimes. When simultaneous charging did occur, crimes of sexual penetration tended to occur in conjunction with other types of sexual penetration charges, the exception being child pornography, which included charges for rape almost half the time. For nonsexual crimes, assault charges more frequently accompanied sex offense charges than homicide for all subcategories of sex offenses. Moreover, no specific type of sex offender appears to escalate to more violent behavior. Perceptions of a relationship between child molestation, pedophilia, or hebophilia and homicide appear to be greatly exaggerated. Persons who sexually penetrate children or teens do not appear to kill with great frequency. Neither do those who sexually victimize adults. . . .

Findings suggest sex offenders do not commit homicide more frequently than other types of offenders. In fact, few murder their victims when committing a sexual assault, and rarely do sex offenders commit homicide in the future. To this end, the assumption of a strong association between sex offending and homicide does not comport to the realities seen by law enforcement, which may have implications for sex offender policies achieving at least one of their goals.

Other types of offenders . . . are rearrested for a homicide in greater proportions than sex offenders, and . . . are not subjected to registration or notification laws.

Legislators likely had many goals in mind when passing sex offender policies. A reduction in the public's fear of sexual victimization and prevention of sexual assault were most likely intended. Registration, notification, and global tracking laws, however, were enacted after incidents of sexually related child homicides were committed. The prevention of homicide, particularly against children, was then also most likely a goal of these sex offender laws as well, but the degree to which these laws have prevented child homicides remains unknown. Although the legislation may well create a reduction in offending, it is also possible that the laws have no effect on behavior or create only minimal reductions at best.

Limits of Current Policies

Current sex offender policies, such as registration, notification, and global tracking, only address sex offenders who have previously been convicted of sex crimes. They can do little to prevent the first-time offender from sexually assaulting or murdering a child. More important, sex offenders are not the only crime type to kill their victims. This study suggests that other types of offenders, such as burglars and robbers, are re-arrested for a homicide in greater proportions than sex offenders, and these offenders are not subjected to registration or notification laws. In this sense, sex offender laws, if applied to only sex offenders, will be missing many other types of offenders who may be just as likely, if not more, to commit murder. To the degree that homicide prevention is a goal of sex offender registration, notification, and global tracking, legislators may want to consider expanding current policies to include other crime types exhibiting a propensity for murder. The legal, constitutional, and financial ramifications of such an expansion, however, would have to be considered.

One possible consequence of such an expansion may be a reduction in the efficacy and effectiveness of sex offender laws. As more offenders and behaviors are added to sex offender policies, it seems possible that it would become more difficult for law enforcement to track and monitor the whereabouts of offenders and apprehend registration violators. For example, under Illinois 1986 registration statute, 3,609 offenders were potentially subject to registration, based on the 1990 arrest data. After the 1995 extension of the laws to include child pornographers, juvenile prostitution pimps and patrons, and sex offenders with adult victims, the number grew to 5,483, an increase of 52%. An increase of this size likely spreads law enforcement thin across a larger population. To this end, if policy makers wish to reduce the risk of violent sexual victimization, particularly against children, and prevent future acts of murder, they may want to consider either limiting the application of registration, notification, and global satellite tracking to offenders who are assessed as posing the greatest risk to society or providing the police, courts, and corrections with the additional resources needed to enforce their expanded expectations, which would be quite a costly endeavor.

Assumptions about people and behaviors do not always comport to empirical reality.

Scholars have [in 2000] warned of the consequences of expanding sex offender policies to more people and behaviors. In their examination of sex offender recidivism [in 2000, K. Soothill, B. Francis, B. Sanderson, and E. Ackerley] discuss the dangers of exaggerating the risk of sexual reoffending to an ever-increasing population of offenders. They state that "potential outcomes of such exaggeration may be to unnecessarily increase the fear of the public, hinder the genuine rehabilitation of offenders who have changed their. ways, while wasting valuable resources on those who do not need increased surveillance." It is possible that public safety would be better served and the public's fear put more at ease by applying sex offender policies to individual offenders based on their specific likelihood of reoffending. After offenders undergo psychological evaluations, and their level of risk identified, registration and community notification could then be mandated for the offenders who pose the greatest risk to public safety based on clinical assessments rather than legislative decree. To some degree, this process is already occurring in some states.

Track Offenders Based on Risk

Although all states require accused sex offenders to register on their convictions, some states have taken to notifying the public as to the whereabouts of these offenders only if they are classified as a high risk for reoffending based on clinical assessments. For instance, Nebraska makes public only the names and addresses of those sex offenders assessed as Level 3 or high risk for recidivating. Washington and Arizona only notify the public as to the residences of offenders assessed at Level 2, or intermediate, and Level 3, high risk. Although New York notifies the public as to all registered sex offenders regardless of their risk levels, this state uses clinical assessments to determine the duration of sex offenders' registration. Offenders classified as Level 1 or Level 2 risk (low or moderate risk, respectively) must only register for 10 years, whereas offenders classified as high risk (Level 3) must register for life. There remains considerable debate surrounding the reliability with which clinical assessments can accurately predict offenders' likelihood of reoffending, but this has not stopped some states from using these assessments to determine which offenders pose the greatest danger to society and informing the public as to their whereabouts. Given the empirical evidence presented here, it seems that these states are on the right track and should possibly even move to registering only those assessed as high risk rather than spending countless hours registering and tracking offenders who pose the least risk to society.

Overall, this study serves to illustrate that assumptions about people and behaviors do not always comport to empirical reality. These assumptions most likely have implications for policies achieving their intended goals. To this end, there is a need to investigate legislative assumptions prior to enacting law. Although this may increase the time between events and the passage of legislation to address them, public safety may benefit in the long term. If policies are enacted based on sound investigation rather than in haste and passion, they may have a better chance of actually achieving at least some of the goals for which they were intended.

CHAPTER 2

Is Treatment for Sex Offenders Effective?

Chapter Preface

The primary goal of sex offender treatment is to increase public safety by reducing the likelihood of repeat offenses. Progress toward meeting this goal, according to some authorities, is compromised by a lack of adequate research, funding, and public support for offender treatment, and a shortage of mental health professionals who are willing and able to treat this population. In addition, treatment experts cite failure to reach a consensus on the most effective approaches to offender treatment, and the low success rates achieved by many treatment programs, as factors complicating advances in the treatment of sex offenders.

One of the most difficult tasks faced by law enforcement and mental health professionals is determining which sex offenders are likely to benefit from treatment and which pose the greatest risk of re-offending. Strategies for assessing offenders' threat to public safety are widely debated, and research conducted on risk assessment has yielded conflicting results. Studies that have compared recidivism (re-offense) rates have been faulted because they include only data on offenders who have been arrested, tried, and convicted of repeated sexual assaults. Since the majority of sexual assaults still go unreported, convicted offenders who have committed further crimes without being caught are not included in the statistics. The range of crimes classified as sex offenses and differences between offenders' access to and participation in treatment makes both determining and analyzing the effectiveness of treatment even more difficult.

Most experts agree that the desire to commit sex offenses cannot be cured, but opinions vary on the extent to which treatment can reduce offenders' urges to act. Mental health professionals are required to provide law enforcement with information that their clients disclose regarding crimes they have committed; therefore, offenders are unlikely to seek out treatment, and those who do enter treatment may not relate anything incriminating about their own behavior. Therapists are thus denied access to potentially crucial information for assessing their clients' risk of commiting future crimes. Offenders who do not confess to all of their crimes are prevented from taking responsibility for their actions.

Assuming personal responsibility for their actions, developing empathy for their victims, and developing strategies to curb their urges to commit further sexual assaults, are essential components of cognitive-behavioral therapy, the preferred approach for treating sex offenders. Despite some promising results from treatment programs, including those that emphasize a community approach to offender treatment, many sex offenders go without treatment or are unable to combat their urges to commit sexual assault. Nevertheless, Linda Grossman, who studies treatment of sex offenders at the University of Illinois at Chicago, has asserted that it is still important to offer treatment. Some surveys have indicated as much as a 30 percent reduction in recidivism among offenders who receive treatment. Grossman has observed that "we treat diseases with higher relapse rates than that. A [study published in 2001] on manic depression found a 38 percent relapse reduction with lithium. But any psychiatrist in the world will treat bipolar disorder with lithium." Furthermore, the Association for the Treatment of Sexual Abusers (ATSA)'s list of the "Ten Things You Should Know about Sex Offenders and Treatment" states that "lifestyle circumstances can affect the chances of new offenses. Stable housing and employment, healthy social and leisure activities, a vigilant and pro-social support system, and ongoing treatment are all important to ensure success," and that "despite its effectiveness, treatment is only one component of an effective strategy to protect the community from sex offenders. Monitoring and support by community corrections agents, other professionals, the offender's social support system, and the entire community play a crucial role."

Treating Sex Offenders Makes Sense

Pamela D. Schultz

Pamela D. Schultz is the author Not Monsters: Analyzing the Stories of Child Molesters, *and an associate professor of communication studies at Alfred University.*

The hunt for released sex offenders, in particular child molesters, has become a moral panic, a mass-mediated wave of irrational public fear. Public policy is based on the idea that child molesters lurk in every neighborhood, playground, schoolyard and public park.

In Suffolk County, [New York,] for instance, a law banning sex offenders from living less than a quarter-mile from places where children congregate has [in December 2006] been joined by legislation limiting the placement of registered sex offenders to one per dwelling and requiring that victims or guardians be informed when an offender eludes his probation officer. [As of December 2006, t]here is also a proposal being floated to conduct random address checks.

In Albany, [New York,] the State Legislature is wrestling with a bill that would send the worst sex offenders to psychiatric facilities at the end of their prison sentence. At the federal level, [in the summer of 2006] the Adam Walsh Protection Act of 2006 expanded the federal Sex Offender Registry, instituted broad levels of Internet surveillance and increased the penalties for child sexual abuse.

Twenty-one states—including New York—use GPS [global positioning system] tracking to keep an eye on offenders. Some, such as Florida, Missouri, Ohio and Oklahoma, require lifetime monitoring, even after a sentence has expired.

Pamela D. Schultz, "Treatment of Sex Offenders Can Protect Community," *Newsday*, December 3, 2006, p. A60. Reproduced by permission of the author.

Policy Based on Faulty Assumptions

By ordinary standards of civil rights in this country, even for convicted criminals, these are radical measures. They stem from the perception that we are inundated with sex offenders and that all convicted child molesters are habitual, violent and predatory, on the prowl for their next victims.

The reality, painful as it is, falls far short of that.

To protect children and prevent future victims, we need to use notification and monitoring to supplement treatment programs, not to supplant them.

As of Sept. 30, [2006,] there were 8,752 Level 2 offenders (moderate risk) and 5,868 Level 3 offenders (highest risk) on New York State's Sex Offender Registry—in a total population of more than 19 million. Child molesters cannot be hiding beneath every rock; there aren't enough of them.

The problem is manageable, given time and resources. We need to calm the hysteria, however, if we want to effectively combat the crime.

Community notification, GPS devices and residency restrictions might be aimed at making communities safer, but unless we use them wisely, they may actually create a more dangerous environment because they stem from unrealistic stereotypes.

First, most convicted child molesters are not dirty old men lurking in playgrounds or sociopaths who randomly kidnap and kill their victims. Physically violent abusers who prey on strangers are the minority. Research shows that 90 percent of child molestation occurs within families or by someone the victim already knows.

By focusing all our attention on 10 percent of the offenders, we ignore a more likely source of danger to our children: potential predators closer to home—fathers, mothers, siblings, friends.

More Effective Approaches Are Available

Second, such stopgap measures as community notification and GPS may seem economical in the short run, but they divert attention from more effective ways to avoid repeat offenses. Contrary to popular perception, for example, convicted sex offenders actually have lower rates of recidivism than other offenders.

When offenders are released, communities need to support offenders with opportunities for continued therapy.

According to the National Center on Institutions and Alternatives, untreated sex offenders sentenced to prison have a recidivism rate of 18.5 percent, compared with around 25 percent for drug offenses and 30 percent for violent offenses.

Intense psychological counseling has been shown to lower sex offenders' recidivism quite effectively. Although treatment cuts recidivism of rapists by a few percent, treatment can cut the rate of recidivism in child molesters by up to one half.

New York State has a six-month in-prison sex offender treatment program that serves more than 1,000 each year. But this should be just the first step in what needs to be a lifetime of treatment.

The reality is that most offenders will be released into the community. If the intent is to protect children and prevent future victims, we need to use notification and monitoring to supplement treatment programs, not to supplant them.

When offenders are released, communities need to support offenders with opportunities for continued therapy. Not only does intensive treatment work, it can be significantly less expensive for taxpayers than long-term incarceration.

It costs about $22,000 per year, excluding treatment, to incarcerate an offender. Community supervision and treatment can cost between $5,000 and $15,000 per year.

But community-based treatment programs can save more than just money. When communities reject convicted offenders by isolating them or driving them to disappear from the system, the price may be paid in potential victims.

Rehabilitate Rather than Ostracize Offenders

There are various hypotheses as to what motivates child molesters, but generally experts agree that offenders tend to exhibit problems with self-esteem, loneliness and depression. The FBI divides child molesters into two groups: preferential and situational offenders. Preferential offenders have a fixed attraction to children. Situational offenders molest children during periods of intense stress and frustration.

Many convicted child molesters fit the situational category. Imagine the psychological pressure on such a convicted child molester who moves into a neighborhood and is greeted by a public outcry. Despised and alienated, the offender might be driven back to the behavior that once brought him comfort.

If we wish to use community notification, GPS and residency requirements as a means of preventing sex offenders' behavior rather than merely as additional forms of punishment, then we must use these tools to help rehabilitate, not ostracize them.

Many of the offenders I have interviewed say they welcome monitoring because they know they need help to control their behavior. If the purpose of monitoring and notification is to pinpont those moments when the offenders need outside help, these tools can truly add to the community's safety.

As a mother, and a sexual abuse survivor, I understand the source of our fear when it comes to child molesters. But paranoia and misinformation will not protect our children.

As one incarcerated child molester observed to me, "I know I need help. I'm going to get out soon. If Megan's Law and monitoring meant that people could keep an eye on me, to help me help myself, then I'd be all for it. But instead, I feel like I'm going to have to hide, and in the end, that's not going to help anybody."

Treatment for Pedophiles Reduces Victimization

Douglas J. Edwards

Douglas J. Edwards is the managing editor of Behavioral Health Management.

Emotions run high when discussing pedophilia. The behavior is so disturbing that it's often attributed to a moral flaw that must be punished. Although the victim's perspective *cannot* be dismissed when examining this psychiatric disorder, is there no hope for helping people who struggle with—and even act on—their desires?

Noted pedophilia expert Fred S. Berlin, MD, PhD, PA, of Johns Hopkins' Department of Psychiatry and Behavioral Sciences, believes that many people with pedophilia can indeed be successfully treated. Yet he says the mental health community's interest in this area has been limited because of the intense stigma attached to pedophilia. "Unfortunately, there are many within mental health who feel that the 'real' mental illnesses are the ones that ought to be treated and that somehow pedophilia, the paraphilias, and the other sexual disorders aren't as deserving," explains Dr. Berlin, who is also the director of the National Institute for the Study, Prevention and Treatment of Sexual Trauma.

Such attitudes—both among mental health professionals and members of society—have led to many common misperceptions about people with pedophilia ("pedophile" itself is a stigmatizing term akin to using "schizophrenic" to describe a person with schizophrenia, Dr. Berlin believes, and for this article the author has avoided using it). Dr. Berlin discounts the common view that pedophilia is a conscious choice. He regards pedophilia as a lifelong sexual orientation, just as hetero- and homosexuality, and he says patients can be terrified by the discovery of pedophilic cravings: "In growing up we discover the kinds of partners to whom we are attracted, and someone's discovering that he is sexually attracted to children is one of the most disturbing and troubling self-revelations that one can come up with."

Pedophilic feelings also have been observed to develop in individuals that previously did not have them, Dr. Berlin notes. For example, some people have developed such cravings after a traumatic brain injury, yet denied having them before.

Types of Pedophilia

Although most cases of pedophilia involve men, people with pedophilia are hardly a homogeneous group; all they share is an attraction to children, explains Dr. Berlin, adding that some are attracted to children of the same sex (homosexual pedophilia), the opposite sex (heterosexual pedophilia), or both sexes (bisexual pedophilia). Their sexual interests might only involve children (exclusive pedophilia) or could involve adults (men, women, or both), as well (nonexclusive pedophilia). People with pedophilia have varying personality types and character traits, he adds.

Compared to studies of other mental health disorders, studies on pedophilia are few and far between in the medical literature.

People with pedophilia, therefore, come from many different life situations—and some are mental health professionals themselves. Take the case of Eugene Hepola, a 72-year-old retired forensic psychologist from Findlay, Ohio. After chatting online for nine months with an FBI agent posing as a 12-year-old girl, Hepola was arrested as he waited for "her" in a Cleveland suburb, reported Cleveland's daily newspaper, *The Plain*

Dealer. Eleven times he sent the "girl" pornography, including video clips of minors having sex. He is now serving three years in prison.

We know so little about this disorder and the people it afflicts because of the paucity [scarcity] of research in this area, says Dr. Berlin. He says factors hindering investigations include stigma (one researcher wouldn't comment for this article because of past negative experiences with the media), challenges in fundraising, and the inability to conduct double-blind studies (researchers can't justify giving a placebo to someone with pedophilic tendencies). Compared to studies of other mental health disorders, studies on pedophilia are few and far between in the medical literature. A recent MEDLINE search for "pedophilia" yielded fewer than 20 results since 2003, compared with hundreds of reports on schizophrenia and depression within that time frame.

Social Stigma Limits Research

David A. D'Amora, MS, LPC, CFC, chair of the Association for the Treatment of Sexual Abusers' Public Policy Committee, says researching topics such as pedophilia can be hampered by basing investigations on approved diagnostic criteria and definitions: "There is, in fact, a significant amount of research on assessment and treatment of folks convicted of sexual offenses. One of the issues is whether one limits oneself to the diagnostic category of pedophilia. The DSM [*Diagnostic and Statistical Manual of Mental Disorders*] diagnoses are not always fully helpful in understanding the issues of sexual violence." For example, a man who molests his son might not meet the criteria for a diagnosis of pedophilia, but he would still be considered a threat to his child. D'Amora adds that much of the current research comes from countries other than the United States, such as Canada, largely because U.S. government funding for studies of sexual offenses and disorders has been limited. The U.S. Department of Justice, however, does sponsor the Center for Sex Offender Management, which offers many resources on the topic.

Although awash with information on other mental health disorders, the Internet offers little for people suffering with pedophilia who are looking for help (the Web, of course, is also a tempting source of illegal child pornography). The first ten results from a recent Google search for "pedophilia" offered little for someone looking for assistance, but searches for "depression" and "schizophrenia" turned up many resources.

John Grohol, PsyD, publisher of PsychCentral.com, says the lack of information on the Web can be tied to the stigma surrounding pedophilia: "I've come across a real bias against people with this problem, both from other mental health professionals and from others looking for mental health support online for other diagnoses. Most folks just don't understand or appreciate the mental health aspect of pedophilia—that the behavioral health field has recognized this as a real disorder in need of real treatment." He adds, "Education can go a long way to helping both professionals and individuals understand that people diagnosed with this disorder need treatment, too. I'm not sure the Internet is helping in that respect right now, given the paucity of unbiased, legitimate information available. Hopefully that will change in the future."

Effective Treatments Are Available

Despite this knowledge gap, Dr. Berlin suggests that effective treatments for pedophilia do exist, although he acknowledges these are not cures: "[Pedophilia] can't be cured any more than alcoholism can be cured, but that doesn't mean either one of those can't be successfully treated." He believes the psychological approach to pedophilia should be similar to the way in which therapists help patients resist cravings for alcohol, heroin, or cocaine. "Part of the successful treatment for both alcoholism and pedophilia is for individuals to recognize that they have an enduring vulnerability and that they must exercise daily vigilance against giving in to unacceptable temptations and falling into unacceptable behavioral patterns," he explains.

Regardless of mental health providers' approaches to pedophilia treatment, if cravings have been acted on, society prefers prison time as the remedy.

Following this logic, Dr. Berlin finds group therapy—often used for substance abuse patients—to be particularly helpful. He says this setting allows participants to share concerns in a safe environment and to discuss strategies for managing their condition, such as not moving into a neighborhood with a high concentration of children and recognizing that sexual temptations will develop if relationships with children become emotionally involved.

Dr. Berlin doesn't put too much stock in aversion therapies designed to alter sexual interests because, he says, evidence supporting their long-term effectiveness is poor. Others do support using such therapies, however.

On the pharmacologic treatment side, the biologic basis of pedophilia remains elusive, admits Dr. Berlin, but he notes that testosterone-lowering medications can be used to reduce males' sexual appetites.

D'Amora, however, warns providers not to think their experience with managing other mental illnesses automatically transfers to the treatment of sexual disorders. "Most people in the traditional behavioral health or mental health field just weren't given the specific training and knowledge regarding the [sex offender] population," he says. He reminds providers to not be limited by DSM diagnoses and to try to acquire the proper education: "It's important that people get the necessary training and understanding as they delve into this. You can't simply subsume the problem of sexual violence under any one or series of diagnoses."

Prison Time Is an Incomplete Solution

Regardless of mental health providers' approaches to pedophilia treatment, if cravings have been acted on, society prefers prison time as the remedy. Dr. Berlin sees this as an incomplete way to handle these offenders, because prisons traditionally have not offered much treatment—and most prisoners eventually are released: "There's nothing about being in prison that can erase a person's attraction to children or enhance that person's capacity to successfully resist acting upon urges." Effective management of this problem requires collaboration between mental health/public health and the justice system, he argues: "As with drug addiction and alcoholism, pedophilia and the other paraphilia disorders are every bit as much a public health problem as they are a criminal justice matter. To best serve society's interests, in my opinion, we have to attend to both of those components. We need not only the attorney general's support, but also the surgeon general's support, if we are really going to deal with these matters in the most effective possible fashion."

Once their time has been served, sexual offenders can be subject to several types of justice system responses aimed at ensuring the community's safety:

- Registering with law enforcement

- Notifying the community of their presence

- Involuntary civil commitment

- Castration (for males)

- Mandated outpatient treatment

Drs. Berlin and D'Amora have no major issues with making sex offenders register with local police, because the justice system already keeps records of criminals' histories. Community notification, however, can be problematic, says Dr. Berlin, because citizens often don't know what to do with the information. Sometimes community notification hinders a sex offender's ability to get a "fresh start," traumatizes the offender's family members, or possibly "outs" the victim, D'Amora and Dr. Berlin note.

The community will be safer only if [sex offenders] can have access to effective treatments.

Civil rights issues regarding community notification have been raised, as well. In perhaps an extreme case, a Texas judge ordered sex offenders to place signs in their yards that read, "Danger! Registered Sex Offender Lives Here," and bumper stickers on their cars that said, "Danger! Registered Sex Offender in Vehicle." Dr. Berlin says the jury is still out on whether community notification will prove to be effective public policy.

D'Amora says that community notification needs at least to be combined with appropriate education. For example, he says, if information on people who have committed sexual offenses is listed on the Web, it should include information on the specific crimes so that the community can understand the level of risk associated with each person. He emphasizes the importance of not scaring the community or giving the false impression that knowing such information makes community members safe.

Treatment or Punishment?

Civil commitment is a particular concern for many mental health providers, says Dr. Berlin. Some states mandate prison inmates to civil commitment if they are determined to still be a threat to society when their prison terms are completed. These laws have survived a U.S. Supreme Court challenge. Under civil commitment, sex offenders receive treatment until they are deemed to be fit for community reintegration, but they can be held indefinitely in institutions such as mental health hospitals. "There has been criticism that this is really just a ruse," notes Dr. Berlin, "that we are really using mental health diagnoses and personnel as a means of preventive detention."

Others have been concerned about civil commitment's effect on the nation's already strained behavioral healthcare system. "There's been a lot of resistance within the mental health community. There have been concerns that this is going to take resources, money, and personnel away from the 'real' mental health issues," explains Dr. Berlin, who argues that all mental health disorders deserve providers' attention.

Mandated chemical or physical castration concerns Dr. Berlin because most states don't require psychiatric evaluations or patient consent for these procedures. If both those conditions are met, says Dr. Berlin, some people may benefit from this intervention—but not all, because castration cannot change a person's underlying personality or sexual orientation.

Many sex offenders are required to attend treatment as a condition of probation or parole, which is how Dr. Berlin sees many of his patients. He believes a more treatment-focused solution is preferable. "We keep thinking we can legislate or punish the problem away, rather than taking a serious look at it from the mental health perspective," he says. "Like it or not, sooner or later, even with civil commitment, even with longer sentencing, the overwhelming majority of sex offenders— including many with pedophilia—are back out in the community. The community will be safer only if they can have access to effective treatments."

Re-Offense Rate Is Exaggerated

Dr. Berlin's own research, involving more than 400 men treated for pedophilia, revealed a less than 8% recidivism rate after five years (with the primary treatment being group therapy). "The common public misperception that most of these people will quickly be back into trouble simply was not true once we looked at this in a fairly objective fashion," says Dr. Berlin, who is working on obtaining even longer follow-up data.

Commenting on people who have committed sexual offenses in general, D'Amora agrees that views on recidivism have been skewed: "When you look at recidivism rates, contrary to what the public understands—or has been told—recidivism rates are generally rather low. It's not true that the majority of sex offenders recidivate." He adds, "It's the people you don't know about—who haven't been arrested, who aren't listed on the Web—who statistically pose a greater risk."

Of course, the risk remains that some people will reoffend. Dr. Berlin says that "the best favor we can do a prospective victim is to keep him or her from being victimized in the first place, and we can only do that by learning more about conditions such as pedophilia, which can predispose individuals to cause suffering in others." But will behavioral healthcare and society-at-large invest the necessary resources? Dr. Berlin hopes so: "It's imperative for society's sake that mental health be much more involved in this situation."

Treating Sex Offenders Is a Waste of Resources

John Florez

John Florez is the founder of several Hispanic civil rights organizations and has served on the staff of Senator Orrin Hatch.

The discussion about sex-offender treatment reminds me of the question: How many social workers does it take to change a light bulb? Only one, but it really has to want to change. Utah's criminal justice system is different. Judges and the Board of Pardons can order sex-offender treatment even if an offender doesn't want it.

The Legislature has its work cut out on this one. Maybe it could start by asking two fundamental questions: Is the Department of Corrections in the business of running sex-offender treatment programs or is it in the business of protecting society? How does society justify paying for offenders' treatment when their victims are left to fend for themselves?

There is a growing number of sex offenders sent to prison. The Department of Corrections officials will be asking the Legislature for an additional $1.2 million for the sex offender-treatment program. According to corrections, there is a waiting list of 1,000 who have been ordered to complete the prison's program that has only 220 spaces and takes 18 months. It seems the courts and Board of Pardons have placed an undue burden on corrections and created a Catch-22.

Costs vs. Benefits of Offender Treatment

Rather than asking for more money to do more of the same, corrections might review its sex offender-treatment program in light of its core purpose, to protect the public. Where is the

John Florez, "Sex-Offender Therapy Is a Waste of Resources," *Deseret Morning News* (Salt Lake City), July 18, 2005. Copyright © 2005 The Deseret News Publishing Co. Reproduced by permission.

justification for 18 months of treatment for the offender, when average citizens can't even afford treatment? Maybe the question Robert McNamara asked in managing the Pentagon applies here: Why use a $50 hammer to do a job when a $10 one would work just as well?

Corrections is the resting place for the problems created by the justice system, including the courts and Board of Pardons, who seem to think treatment is the answer and are quick to order sex offenders to complete a treatment program. Many in the justice system see therapy as the panacea to helping offenders whether they want it or not.

But basic to helping people is that they first have to realize they have a problem. Some professionals believe sex offenders are driven by their compulsive urges and deny they have a problem. Thus, ordering offenders to get treatment is a waste of resources. Some may simply agree to put their name on the long waiting list so they can successfully complete the 18-month program required by the Board of Pardons. Upon completion of the program, how is success measured? Should it not be that offenders stop committing sex crimes? How can that be determined in a lock-up facility?

I once asked a psychiatrist friend, "What works in the treatment of sex offenders?" He replied he did not know, but he could tell me what doesn't work. Though prison officials claim great success for their program, they are relying on self-studies. According to one of them, those that had treatment returned to prison for a sex offense less than those that had no treatment. That's like the thesis I did to complete graduate school. It was a study to determine the value of social workers in a surgical ward. I proved that they were valuable, and guess who was the social worker?

Alternatives to Therapy

Corrections might find more efficient ways to carry out its mission rather than building a backlog for its treatment program. At the same time, judges and the Board of Pardons must also re-evaluate their treatment recommendations. Perhaps money could best be used to provide the courts with better assessments in the sentencing of offenders. Who is to say that incarcerating some sex offenders for a short time, as a shock, and then retuning them to their communities with intensive supervision might not be more effective? Especially offenders who are established members of their communities where the shame could provide valuable social control. In addition, the development of new drugs to manage and alter human behavior is now showing promise in dealing with addictions and compulsions prevalent in sex offenders. Rather than putting out more money for therapy, maybe it could best be used to pay more, and hire more, correctional officers to manage offenders in prison and in the community. Last, but not least, why not give all of the collected restitution money to victims, instead of corrections taking a portion for its administration.

Maybe the $10 tool rather than the $50 one might work just as well.

Pedophiles Are Criminals, Not Patients

Thomas S. Szasz

Thomas S. Szasz is Professor Emeritus of psychiatry at State University of New York Health Science Center in Syracuse, New York. Although he is not a member of the Church of Scientology, he is a proponent of Scientology's antipsychiatric organizations, is openly critical of the use of medicine for the purposes of social control, and is well known for his 1960 book, The Myth of Mental Illness.

In the long history of priests sexually abusing children, perpetrators and victims play the principal parts. However, there are two other important players in this drama, only one of which—the priests' superiors, who ignored and indeed facilitated the crimes of their subordinates—have received attention.

But the identity, the very existence, of the other accomplices—the psychiatrists and psychiatric institutions that "diagnose" and "treat" priests who, in fact, are criminals—has been overlooked. Why? Because they are an integral part of our love affair with medicalizing life and replacing responsibility with "therapy."

The tragedy of pedophilia begins, as do many modern tragedies, by people stupefying themselves by confusing their own tongue, re-enacting God's punishment of mankind at Babel. An adult who uses a child for his sexual gratification is a kind of rapist: He is guilty of the crime of assault. Such a person is a criminal, not a patient.

A History of Turning Behaviors into Diseases

How does medicine—talkmg about diseases and treatments—enter into this affair? The same way it enters into our belief that other (mis)behaviors are diseases, amenable to treatment—through psychiatry. It's a long story that can be condensed into a few sentences. For millennia, masturbation, homosexuality, and the many other non-heterosexual, nonprocreative uses of the genital organs were considered to be grievous sins and were prevented and punished accordingly.

Viewing "pedophilia" as an illness, like pneumonia, implies that the subject is not responsible for it and it is treatable.

Toward the end of the 19th century, they started becoming "mental" diseases. This process played an important part in the transformation of mad-doctoring as quackery into modern psychiatry as a bona fide branch of medicine.

Creating diseases by coining disease-sounding terms was raised to the level of a psychiatric art form by Baron Richard von Krafft-Ebing (1840-1902), a German-born psychiatrist who was professor of psychiatry at the Universities of Strasbourg, Graz and Vienna. The work that made Krafft-Ebing world famous is "Psychopathia Sexualis," the first edition of which appeared in 1886. Sexology became an integral part of medicine—and the new science of psychiatry—by physicians authoritatively renaming sexual sins "sexual perversions" and declaring them to be "cerebral neuroses" (Krafft-Ebing).

Lawyers, politicians and the public embraced this transformation as the progress of science, rather than dismissing it as medical megalomania based on nothing more than the manipulation of language.

Yet, Krafft-Ebing himself acknowledged that what he was doing had nothing to do with science. It had to with "compassion." He wrote: "The physician finds, perhaps, a solace in the fact that he may at times refer those manifestations which offend against our ethical and aesthetical principles to a diseased condition of the mind or the body. . . . He can save the honor of humanity in the forum of morality, and the honor of the individual before the judge and his fellow-men."

Sigmund Freud extended Krafft-Ebing's psychopathologizing from sexual behavior to everyday behavior. In "The Psychopathology of Everyday Life" (1901), he inverted William Shakespeare's humanistic interpretation of conflict as an integral part of life into a dehumanized interpretation of tragedy as a manifestation of psychopathology.

Sexual Assault Is a Horrific Crime

At the root of the confusion about pedophilia lies the term "sex crime." Exemplified by rape, so-called sex crimes are particularly heinous types of assault. But assaults that result in blinding the victim or rendering him paraplegic are also heinous, but we do not, on that account, call them "eye crimes" or "neurological crimes." The belief that sex crimes are "special" paves the way for the delusion that they are diseases, a false belief psychiatrists turn into "reality" by naming what were formerly perversions "paraphilias" (hemophilia, necrophilia, pedophilia, zoophilia).

I contend that psychiatrists . . . are, like the pedophilic priests' superiors, accomplices to their crimes.

This is factually erroneous and morally wicked, because sexually assaulting a child is not a disease (just as homosexuality was never a disease), and because viewing "pedophilia" as an illness, like pneumonia, implies that the subject is not responsible for it and it is treatable. In turn, these beliefs lead to excusing the behavior and engaging in a pseudomedical charade of treating it. The result is that psychiatrists and psychiatric institutions become accomplices to pedophilia, especially by priests.

According to press reports, "centers used by the Catholic Church today include the Johns Hopkins clinic, the Institute of Living and the Menninger Foundation in Topeka, Kans., according to those who treat pedophilic priests. For the most part, the regimen for treating pedophilia involves individual and group therapy to break down denial and a 12-step program, similar to the Alcoholics Anonymous model, to help control sexual addictions."

That is the psychiatrists' version of such programs. The clergy's version, judging by their actions, is that such programs provide safe houses for sexually misbehaving priests, where they can be hidden until they are quietly reassigned to ply their trade elsewhere.

Offenders and Their Accomplices

Fred Berlin, the founder of the Johns Hopkins Sexual Disorders Clinic, is quoted as saying that pedophilic patients are closely monitored after being discharged from a program. However, pedophilic priests are criminals who should be imprisoned, not monitored by psychiatrists paid off for their collusion by the Catholic Church.

I contend that psychiatrists—especially the authors of the influential *Diagnostic and Statistical Manual of Mental Disorders*, published in periodically revised editions by the American Psychiatric Association—are, like the pedophile priests' superiors, accomplices to their crimes. Their offense is classifying and treating pedophilia as a disease. In the absence of that deception, tragedies such as the Catholic Church and the victims now face could not come into being.

A Boston news Web site reported: "A.W. Richard Sipe, a psychotherapist and former monk who counseled sexually disordered priests in the 1970s and 1980s at the Seton Psychiatric

Institute and the Johns Hopkins University Sexual Disorders Clinic, recalls: "Oh, Father John Geoghan. He is well known in the circles of those who treat priest pedophiles. He is notorious because he has been treated by so many people, at nearly every psychiatric hospital in the country."

Credo quia absurdum est. [I believe, because it is absurd.]

What Controversies Surround Sex Offender Policy?

Chapter Preface

Nearly all of the sex offender policy issues currently debated—registration, community notification, residency restrictions, civil commitment, classification of juveniles as sex offenders, mandatory sentencing, the death penalty, and castration—involve achieving an effective balance of public safety, maintaining individual civil liberties, and a just and efficient allocation of resources. Those who participate in the public discourse on sex offender policy share a desire to protect children and reduce sexual assault but differ greatly in their opinions about the rights of offenders and their assessment of just and effective punishment and management of sex offenders.

Many lawmakers and political pundits argue that sex offenders' rights are forfeited when they commit crimes against children. They support their arguments by citing cases in which repeat offenders have assaulted and murdered children after they have been released from prison; for such offenders, these commentators argue, no punishment is too harsh and no price is too high. On the other side of the debate, civil libertarians and victims' rights advocates, mental health professionals, defense attorneys, and members of the law enforcement community assert that there are too many restrictions placed on too many offenders. This, they say, leads to vigilante violence against offenders whose whereabouts are readily known through public Web sites. Furthermore, opponents of stricter policies argue that such measures result in unfairly harsh penalties for individuals—including juveniles, teens who have engaged in consensual sex, and those arrested for public urination and indecent exposure—who are labeled as sex offenders but pose no threat of violence to their communities. Public safety and federal, state, and local budgets would be better served, they argue, by targeting only those sex offenders who commit forcible sex crimes or demonstrate a tendency toward violence.

A case which illustrates the complexities of the debate over whether current sex offender policies are just and effective is that of Genarlow Wilson, who was sentenced to 10 years in prison without possibility of parole in 2005 after he was videotaped having consensual oral sex with a 15-year-old girl at a 2003 New Years Eve party in Georgia. Oral sex between teens constituted aggravated child molestation and carried a mandatory sentence under a Georgia state law in effect in 2003. Had Wilson engaged in sexual intercourse with the 15-year-old his case would have fallen under a so-called "Romeo and Juliet" exception to the law that would have resulted in a misdemeanor charge. The Georgia law was changed in 2006, and now consensual oral sex between teens is a misdemeanor punishable by a maximum of one year behind bars with no requirement to register as a sex offender, as Wilson will be required to do after he is released from prison. Efforts to appeal Wilson's conviction have been hampered by the party videotape, which depicts Wilson—and several other male partygoers—engaging in sexual intercourse with a 17-year-old girl. Wilson was acquitted of charges of raping the 17-year-old when a jury disagreed with the prosecutor's claim that the girl was only partially conscious and thus unable to give consent. Although Douglas County District David McDade asserted in March 2007 that "six young men basically gang raped a 17-year-old," the other five males arrested in the case accepted plea agreements and never went to trial. Wilson's sentence has been widely criticized, even by members of the jury that convicted him and former state Representative Matt Towery, who sponsored the 1995 law under which Wilson was sentenced to prison. Towery has asserted that "the law was designed to protect kids against really, really bad people doing very bad things" and "was never intended to put kids in jail for oral sex."

Registries and Community Notification Target the Wrong People

Michelle L. Meloy

Michelle L. Meloy is an assistant professor in the department of sociology, anthropology, and criminal justice at Rutgers University, and is the author of Sex Offenses and the Men Who Commit Them.

Sex offender registration laws, designed to assist law enforcement in the investigation of sex crimes, have been in existence [since the mid-1940s]. Community notification mandates are relatively new and are designed to empower citizens by providing them with information about convicted sex offenders in their area. The first community notification legislation was enacted in Washington State in 1990 after the sexual assault and mutilation of a young Tacoma boy by a paroled sex offender, Earl Shriner—who had warned authorities of his continuing fantasies to rape and mutilate children prior to his release from prison. On July 2, 1994, a seven-year-old Hamilton, New Jersey, girl named Megan Kanka was raped and asphyxiated by her thirty-three-year-old neighbor, Jesse Timmendequas. Mr. Timmendequas was a convicted child molester who, along with two other paroled sex offenders, resided near the Kanka family. The brutal nature of this rape and murder hurled the issue of sexual violence against children into the national spotlight. . . . [T]hese brutal attacks against innocent children led to the swift enactment of mandatory registration and community notification, commonly referred to as "Megan's Law." This package of sex offender statutes was pro-

Michelle L. Meloy, "Legal Warfare," *Sex Offenses and the Men Who Commit Them: An Assessment of Sex Offenders on Probation*, Lebanon, NH: Northeastern University Press and University Press of New England, 2006. Copyright © 2006 by Northeastern University Press. All rights reserved. Reproduced by permission.

posed to protect the community, specifically children, by requiring convicted sex offenders to register with their local law enforcement agencies upon conviction or release. Differences exist in sex offender registration and community notification laws because there are no national standards to guide the application of the community notification process.

Sex offenders subjected to community notification were just as likely to be arrested for new sex crimes as they had been before the law was implemented.

Universally, the most sensitive and controversial aspect of the law is community notification, whereby information about the offender's name and residence is available to the public. It is becoming increasingly common for an offender's picture, work address, and residence to be available on the Internet. In some states, highway billboard signs post the sex offender's name, address, and photo under a caption reading something like "Beware: Sex Offender Lives Near You." In other locales, residents can receive a notification in the mail with the sex offender's name and picture listed. In other jurisdictions, such as Delaware, the defendant's driver's license contains a special mark designating him/her as a sexual offender. The invasive labeling of sex offenders is necessary, according to Mrs. Kanka: "If I had known that three sex perverts were living across the street from me, Megan would be alive today."

Public Support for Community Notification Is Overwhelming

Mrs. Kanka is not alone in her belief that a sex offender's information should be accessible to the public. The support for this legislation is demonstrated not only by the swift passage of Megan's Law itself (which the state of New Jersey adopted only weeks after Megan's murder), but also by the fact that within the same year, sixteen other state legislatures had written similar policies. In 1996, the U.S. Congress passed legislation (Jacob Wetterling Act followed by the Pam Lyncher Act) that required all states to provide some form of community notification of convicted sex offenders.

In 1997, then Attorney General Janet Reno stated that federal registration and notification legislation was necessary because "the Bureau of Justice Statistics report shows that accurate registries and effective community notification programs are at the heart of our fight against sex offenders." The contention, however, that sex offender registries are the "heart" of the battle against General Reno cites demonstrates statistical evidence that most sex offenders are *known assailants*, nor the strangers that are the focus of registries. By the next year, all fifty states had sex offender registration and community notification laws. State statutes vary regarding which types of offenders are subject to community notification, the intensity of the notification process, and the sensitivity of offender information made available to the public. Some states require broad dissemination of information about certain tiers of sex offenders to local organizations, community residents, and media (New Jersey, Oregon, and Washington take this approach). A second group of states gives probation and parole officers discretion to notify anyone they choose with information about released sex offenders (Connecticut, Georgia, and New York engage in this practice). A third group authorizes public disclosure of sex offender information for any purpose to any person who submits a written request to the county sheriff or local police. The information provided may be about a named individual or about all registrants in a geographical area (Alaska, Michigan, South Carolina, Vermont, and Virginia follow this directive). . . .

Are We Now Protected from Sex Offenders?

Sex offender registration requires convicted sex offenders to notify law enforcement of their residential status (and any changes) for a specified period of time. Community notification laws make this information available to the public. Not much is understood about the sociological implications or effectiveness of sex offender registration and community notification. A 1988 California study on sex offender registration and recidivism of convicted sex offenders found that mandated registration was effective in helping identify, locate, and arrest suspected sex offenders. The law's impact on sexual recidivism, however, was insignificant; the rate of recidivism among sex offenders and non-sex offenders was not statistically different. In 1995, a study was conducted (in Washington State) on the impact of community notification on sexual re-offending. Once again, researchers found the law produced no statistically significant difference in rearrest rates. Sex offenders subjected to community notification were just as likely to be arrested for new sex crimes as they had been before the law was implemented.

The efficacy of community notification is only compromised by including persons who pose no safety risk to the community on sex offender registries.

There are logistical complications with registration and notification. Collection, maintenance, enforcement, and the notification process are expensive and labor-intensive. Also, lists are likely to be incomplete and inaccurate as offenders change residences frequently or refuse to cooperate—a common problem known as displacement. Because of the stigma associated with community notification, offenders often move to other communities and may not notify officials of the change. An investigation conducted in [1997 in] Tennessee revealed that 28 percent of convicted sex offenders moved from their registered communities and then failed to reregister. Other studies found that registration compliance of convicted sex offenders with law enforcement authorities fared no better than 25 to 54 percent nationally.

A potential unintended consequence of registration and notification mandates are that individuals convicted of consensual acts of sodomy are required to register as sex offenders. In this regard, some contend that community notification statutes reinforce antigay sentiment by mandating registration for sodomy convictions and encouraging police officers to use undercover tactics to apprehend gays. Homophobia's role in sex crime prosecution was an issue with several of the interview respondents who were part of this research. A handful of male sex offenders (those reporting themselves to be gay or bisexual) who agreed to be interviewed said that they were arrested and placed on probation after an Internet sting operation targeting "male only" chat rooms uncovered sexual conversations between themselves and others who self-identified as boys under the age of eighteen. In actuality, the offenders were corresponding with undercover police officers posing as minors.

Homosexuals Are Wrongly Targeted

Despite the widespread belief to the contrary, there is no evidence to suggest that there is any link between homosexuality and criminal sex offending behavior. Given the lack of danger posed by gays and lesbians—and the rarity of stranger-danger—it certainly seems that there are more productive and victim-oriented ways to allocate scarce criminal justice resources. For instance, education platforms targeted to parents and citizens about the typical sex offender profile and victim-offender relationships or increased funding for sex offender treatment programs in prison could be more productive programs. The efficacy of community notification is only compromised by including persons who pose no safety risk to the community on sex offender registries.

We must hope that the practice of registering individuals convicted of consensual acts of sodomy as sex offenders will stop. In June 2003 (*Lawrence v. Texas*), the U.S. Supreme Court ruled all sodomy laws illegal, citing a constitutional right to sexual privacy. This landmark decision reversed a 1986 ruling (*Bowers v. Hardwick*) that restricted some forms of consensual sexual contact between couples even in the privacy of their own homes. It is too soon to predict what the ripple effect of the *Lawrence* decision will have in terms of gay rights in general; at the very least, the thirteen states that still have sodomy laws will no longer be able to selectively prosecute private, consensual homosexual acts and require that these names be on sex offender registration lists. The more accurately registries list dangerous and predatory sex offenders, the more likely they are to identify those who genuinely pose a risk to women and children.

There are historical incidents of antigay sentiments in sex offender legislation as well. One of the factors behind the first wave of sex offender legislation was an alleged association between psychosis and criminality. This purported relationship between psychopathology and crime, coupled with the notion at the time that homosexuality was "caused" by mental illness, resulted in widespread support for sex offender laws in the 1930s. Widespread support for sexual psychopath laws also resulted from the misplaced fear that same-sex conduct was synonymous with pedophilia and that gay men actively "recruited" children for sex. According to one author, the initial wave of sex offender legislation was so saturated with homophobia that it was questionable whether the term "sexual psychopath" was merely another way to say homosexual. It was not until the government surrendered its goal of forging a single definition of sexual morality (and instead prioritized community safety) that sexual psychopath laws were revised, no longer targeting adult consensual same sex relations.

Communities Are Notified About the Wrong People

There are other problems with community notification laws. For example, while notification laws are criticized for being overinclusive, they are concomitantly riddled with problems of being underinclusive in that many offenders are able to avoid registration through plea negotiations. For example, it is common for offenders to enter plea negotiations for offenses that do not carry the registration mandate. A "successful" plea agreement does not negate an offender's potential risk. Many of the non-mandated registrants may be equally dangerous, if not more dangerous, than registered offenders. For example, Richard Allen Davis, the individual convicted in California of the highly publicized sexual assault and murder of Polly Klas, had previously served fifteen years in prison for sex crimes, dating back to 1973. Because of plea negotiations, however, he was able to avoid convictions for the specific sex offenses that would have required him to register. And Leroy Hendricks, the defendant who fought the constitutionality of sexually dangerous persons' civil commitment statutes was himself released from custody many times after accepting plea negotiations for reduced sentences. Furthermore, it must be acknowledged that because sex crimes are severely underreported and few offenders are ever caught, registration legislation applies to only the small percentage of offenders who are identified, apprehended and convicted of committing certain sex crimes.

A "one size fits all" sex offender registration and notification is not in the best interest of social justice or community safety.

Because sex offender registration and community notification target the "stranger" sexual assailant and make no provisions to protect children who fall prey to sexual offenses at the hands of a known assailant, sex offender laws perpetuate an inaccurate image of harm. Estimates indicate that 85 percent of all child sexual abuse (and more than 95 percent of the abuse against children under the age of six) is committed by family members and friends. Sexual victimization data collected on persons twelve years of age and older indicate a similar pattern. Consequently, sex offender registration laws imbue a false sense of security by leading communities into believing they can protect children from sex offenders by keeping them away from the men on these lists. As stated elsewhere, most child molesters are not crazed, savage, beastlike strangers. Rather, many sex offenders hold positions of authority and trust and are relatives, friends, neighbors, or acquaintances of the child. The same holds true for most of the men included in this analysis [my book, *Sex Offenses and the Men Who Commit Them*]. More than 50 percent of the male sex offenders discussed in [my book] have high school diplomas or college degrees and eight out or ten assaulted a relative or someone they already knew. To reiterate: sex offender registration and community notification legislation fails to target the offenders who pose the greatest risk to children (relatives and friends). Therefore, at most it can hope to identify only about 15 percent of unknown offenders. Thus this type of legislation is unlikely to be efficacious at curbing sexual violence in any measurable way.

Shame and Stigma Reduce Safety

Not only is there no empirical evidence that sex offender laws provide for safer communities, questions also remain regarding the overall effect the labeling and public branding of an individual as "sex offender" is likely to have. Because many states now make their sex offender registries accessible to the public on the Internet (and the U.S. Supreme Court has approved the practice), the availability of this information has grown from the confines of a local community to being but a computer stroke away to the entire world. This change in accessibility is likely to increase the degree of public stigmatization felt by offenders. The notification process may further alienate the offender, increasing feelings of detachment and anger and making it more difficult for registered offenders to find housing and employment—thereby enhancing their likelihood of reoffending. "Because low-level offenders pose minimal risk of reoffense, the harms or loss of reputation and anonymity along with the stigma of being branded a sex offender could outweigh the protective value of public notification." Therefore, responsible public policy calls for courts and policymakers to consider the potential harms caused by these laws (including loss of employment, residential stability, loss of support networks) against the potential risks or dangerousness a particular offender poses to the community. Community shaming and stigmatization, without concern for therapeutic reintegration, will likely increase the risks of recidivism. A "one size fits all" sex offender registration and notification is not in the best interest of social justice or community safety.

There is also an increased risk of attack by vigilantes. In the context of sex crimes, vigilantism comes in either the form of ostracism or acts of individual violence and retribution. For instance, according to one report, 26 percent of registered sex offenders are the target of some public harassment; the finding was replicated in [my] research. Specifically, 40 percent of the men on sex offender probation who were interviewed talked openly about their fears and experiences with vigilante justice. Public stigmatization, social isolation, and vigilantism are increased when names and addresses of sex offenders are released into the community. "We're turning [the offender] into a pariah, and creating situations where he is more likely to re-offend," reports Nadine Strossen, president of the American Civil Liberties Union. "Megan's Law is more about politics than it is about public safety." Incidents of vigilante attacks have been reported in Washington, New Jersey, and other locales around the country. At times, these acts of vigilante justice are extreme. For example, in the state of Washington, hours before the highly publicized release of a sex offender, his house was burned to the ground. In the state of New Jersey a released sex offender had his home riddled with bullets after a bulletin was released notifying community members of his presence. "Released sex offenders may find it extremely difficult to re-assimilate into society. Problems finding and maintaining employment, securing housing, and making and keeping social relationships are the inevitable results of the stigma attached to the label 'sex offender.'" [The men interviewed for my book] worried about vigilante justice being imposed on them while they were on probation. In *Doe v. Poritz* (1995) the U.S. Supreme Court stated that they had faith in the public and media's ability to handle sex offender registration information responsibly and nonpunitively.

Iowa's Residency Restrictions Have Proven Unsuccessful

Iowa County Attorneys Association

The Iowa County Attorneys Association issued a statement in December 2006 detailing numerous problems created by a sex offender residency restriction law passed in Iowa, and offering suggestions for alternatives to the law that would more effectively address the public safety concerns that prompted the original legislation.

The Iowa County Attorneys Association [ICAA] believes that the 2,000 foot residency restriction for persons who have been convicted of sex offenses involving minors does not provide the protection that was originally intended and that the cost of enforcing the requirement and the unintended effects on families of offenders warrant replacing the restriction with more effective protective measures.

Iowa's Residency Restrictions Are Ineffective and Costly

> *Efforts to . . . minimize the rate of reoffending . . . are severely impaired by the residency restriction, compromising the safety of children.*

The ICAA has the following observations concerning the current restriction:

1. Research shows that there is no correlation between residency restrictions and reducing sex offenses against children or improving the safety of children.

Iowa County Attorneys Association, "Statement on Sex Offender Residency Restrictions in Iowa," December 11, 2006, www.iowa-icaa.com. Reproduced by permission.

2. Research does not support the belief that children are more likely to be victimized by strangers at the covered locations than at other places.

3. Residency restrictions were intended to reduce sex crimes against children by strangers who seek access to children at the covered locations. Those crimes are tragic, but very rare. In fact, 80 to 90 percent of sex crimes against children are committed by a relative or acquaintance who has some prior relationship with the child and access to the child that is not impeded by residency restrictions. Only parents and caretakers can effectively impede that kind of access.

4. Law enforcement has observed that the residency restriction is causing offenders to become homeless, to change residences without notifying authorities of their new locations, to register false addresses or to simply disappear. If they do not register, law enforcement and the public do not know where they are living. The resulting damage to the reliability of the sex offender registry does not serve the interests of public safety.

5. There is no demonstrated protective effect of the residency requirement that justifies the huge draining of scarce law enforcement resources in the effort to enforce the restriction.

6. The categories of crimes included in the restriction are too broad, imposing the restriction on many offenders who present no known risk to children in the covered locations.

7. A significant number of offenders have married or have been reunited with their victims; and, in those cases, the residency restriction is imposed on the victims as well as the offenders.

8. Many offenders have families whose lives are unfairly and unnecessarily disrupted by the restriction, causing

children to be pulled out of school and away from friends, and causing spouses to lose jobs and community connections.

9. Many offenders are physically or mentally disabled but are prohibited from living with family members or others on whom they rely for assistance with daily needs.

10. The geographic areas included in the prohibited 2,000 foot zones are so extensive that realistic opportunities to find affordable housing are virtually eliminated in most communities. The lack of transportation in areas not covered by the restriction limits employment opportunities. The adoption of even more restrictive ordinances by cities and counties exacerbates the shortage of housing possibilities.

Unintended Negative Effects of Residency Restrictions

11. The residency restriction has no time limit; and, for many offenders, the restriction lasts beyond the requirement that they be listed on the sex offender registry. For this reason, there are many offenders who are subject to the residency restriction but who are not required to inform law enforcement of their place of residence, making enforcement nearly impossible.

12. There is no accommodation in the current statute for persons on parole or probation supervision. These offenders are already monitored and their living arrangements approved. The restriction causes many supervised residential placements to be unavailable even though they may be the most appropriate and safest locations for offenders to live.

13. Many prosecutors have observed that the numerous negative consequences of the lifetime residency restriction has caused a reduction in the number of confessions made by offenders in cases where defendants usu-

ally confess after disclosure of the offense by the child. In addition, there are more refusals by defendants charged with sex offenses to enter into plea agreements. Plea agreements are necessary in many cases involving child victims in order to protect the children from the trauma of the trial process. This unforeseen result seriously jeopardizes the welfare of child victims and decreases the number of convictions of sex offenders to accurate charges. Consequently, many offenders will not be made fully accountable for their acts and will not be required to complete appropriate treatment or other rehabilitative measures that would enhance the safety of children. Similar unintended negative effects often accompany well-intended efforts to increase prison sentences with mandatory provisions.

14. The drastic reduction in the availability of appropriate housing, along with the forced removal of many offenders from established residences, is contrary to well-established principles of treatment and rehabilitation of sex offenders. Efforts to rehabilitate offenders and to minimize the rate of reoffending are much more successful when offenders are employed, have family and community connections, and have a stable residence. These goals are severely impaired by the residency restriction, compromising the safety of children by obstructing the use of the best known corrections practices.

Replace Residency Restrictions with Effective Laws

For these reasons, the Iowa County Attorneys Association supports the replacement of the residency restriction with more effective measures that do not produce the negative consequences that have attended the current statute. For example, the ICAA would support a measure that includes the following:

- A statute creating defined protected areas ("child safe zones") that sex offenders would be prohibited from entering except in limited and safe circumstances. Such areas might include schools and childcare facilities.

- Entrance into the protected areas would be allowed only for activities involving an offender's own child and only with advance notice and approval from those in charge of the location.

- The restriction should cover offenses against "children" (under age 14), rather than "minors" (under 18).

- The statute should specifically preempt local ordinances that attempt to create additional restrictions on sex offenders. Such ordinances result in a variety of inconsistent rules and promote apprehension among local authorities that they must act to defend themselves from the perceived effects of the actions of other communities.

- Most important, any restriction that carries the expectation that it can be effectively enforced must be applied to a more limited group of offenders than is covered by the current residency restriction. This group should be identified by a competent assessment performed by trained persons acting on behalf of the state. The assessment should be directed at applying the statutory restriction only to those offenders that present an actual risk in public areas to children with whom the offender has no prior relationship.

- Children will be safer with clarification and strengthening of certain child sex abuse laws, including, sex abuse by deception, sexual exploitation of a person "reasonably believed to be a minor," using a position of authority to cause children to engage in a sex act, and requiring admission at trial of a defendant's prior acts of sexual abuse.

- Sex offender treatment both inside and outside of prison should be fully funded and improved.

- Measures should be enacted that aim at keeping *all* young people safe from *all* offenders. This should include programs that focus on the danger of abuse that may lie within the child's family and circle of acquaintances. It is important to help children and parents recognize the signs and dangers of sex abuse by persons with ordinary access to children.

- Recognize that child safety from sex offenses is not amendable to simple solutions by creating a Sex Offender Treatment and Supervision Task Force to identify effective strategies to reduce child sex offenses.

These observations of Iowa prosecutors are not motivated by sympathy for those committing sex offenses against children, but by our concern that legislative proposals designed to protect children must be both effective and enforceable. Anything else lets our children down.

The Iowa County Attorneys Association strongly urges the General Assembly and the Governor to act promptly to address the problems created by the 2,000 foot residency restriction by replacing the restriction with measures that more effectively protect children, that reduce the unintended unfairness to innocent persons and that make more prudent use of law enforcement resources, and strengthen the child sex abuse laws and prosecution. The ICAA stands ready to assist in any way with this effort.

GPS Tracking of Sex Offenders Fails to Protect Children and Promotes Panic

Katharine Mieszkowski

Katharine Mieszkowski is a senior writer for Salon.com.

It's not every Election Day that voters can cast a ballot to banish thousands of people to the hinterlands, but Californians did just that [in November 2006] and eagerly so. Seventy percent voted to ban registered sex offenders from living within 2,000 feet of a school or park, effectively outlawing them from many residential areas in the state.

Known as "Jessica's Law," after a 9-year-old Florida girl [Jessica Lunsford] who was kidnapped from her home, sexually abused and murdered by a registered sex offender, the California proposition swept in a myriad of punitive changes. The crackdown on residency applies to all registered sex offenders, including those convicted of a misdemeanor, such as indecent exposure. Most notably, felony sex offenders will now be tracked 24 hours a day, seven days a week, via GPS (global positioning system), even after they're out of prison and off parole. The state senator and advocates behind the proposition call the GPS devices a necessary and vital tool to control sexual criminals.

The California measure makes no distinction between habitual offenders at high risk of striking again, worth having their every move tracked electronically once they're out of prison, and the felons who have served their time and present no apparent threat to public safety in the eyes of the court. Just put a GPS device on all of them, voters said, forever.

Now, the state's government and the courts are puzzling out how to bring the voters' sweeping mandate to life.

Stricter Laws Are Symbolic of National Hysteria

The broad California measure is symptomatic of a national tide of fear about sexual predators lurking in the bushes by the playground, at the mall, just on the other side of the elementary school fence, and skulking about on MySpace. A sort of boogeyman come to life, sex predators even have their own gotcha TV reality show masquerading as a news program, *Dateline's To Catch a Predator*. Every state in the nation now has a sex offender registry, tracking where offenders live. But Virginia, for one, is taking the fight to cyberspace, considering legislation to have offenders register their e-mail addresses and instant-messenger handles, so the Internet can be cleaned up, too.

[Emphasizing] the sexual predator in the schoolyard or on the Internet, can be counterproductive, as resources to fight sexual crimes . . . are misplaced.

But as states rush to impose harsher penalties on sex criminals, critics—legal and criminal analysts, and even some victims of sex crimes themselves—state that the punitive new laws violate civil liberties and are ineffective. And while a technological fix like fastening GPS devices to former felons may make the public feel safer, it will do little to protect the children who are the victims of most sex crimes.

Currently, 23 states use GPS to monitor some sex offenders while they're on parole. The devices, outfitted on an ankle bracelet, are typically placed on offenders considered at high risk of striking again. Because the conditions of parole often restrict where an offender can go, outlawing, say, schools or day-care centers, the device can behave like a 24-hour virtual parole officer, keeping tabs to see if the offender follows the rules. Nobody disputes the use of the technology for those on parole.

But now several states have decided: Why should 24-hour electronic monitoring end with parole? Even after offenders have legally paid their debt to society, the states still want to track their every move, regardless of their risk for recidivism. "We're finding ways to use technology to create what is a permanent deprivation of liberty," says Marc Rotenberg, executive director of the Electronic Privacy Information Center. "It raises some very important issues about what the state may do to an essentially free person."

Current Practices Are Not Based on Reality

Critics declare that sexual crimes committed by predators are a serious problem, and they don't mean to underplay them. But most sexual crimes, especially those committed against children, they point out, happen closer to home and involve somebody whom the victim knew and trusted, like a family member or a neighbor. The incessant emphasis on the boogeyman, the sexual predator in the schoolyard or on the Internet, can be counterproductive, as resources to fight sexual crimes, and public perception of them, are misplaced.

"The reality is the vast majority of registrants are not predatory, and don't pose danger to strangers, which is the only reason GPS would be useful," says Jeff Stein, a criminal defense attorney, and co-chair of the legislative committee for California Attorneys for Criminal Justice. The new GPS devices, he says, fuel "the hysteria that all registrants are predators."

The strict new California proposition was hatched by Los Angeles state Sen. George Runner. He explained the value of GPS in an October TV interview: "Hey, if you are a felony sex offender, we're going to want to know where you are at all times." Once a GPS device is strapped to an offender's ankle, he said, "a law enforcement [officer] can type in their name and see where these individuals have been over a period of time—that's necessary."

Ernie Allen, president of the National Center for Missing and Exploited Children, a nonprofit advocacy group, also believes that GPS devices are necessary. "It's a vital tool for knowing where sex offenders are, and using the full weight of the state to ensure that these offenders are going to their jobs and living where they're supposed to live and doing the things that they're supposed to do," he says. "And if they're not, it's important that authorities know about it."

Every state now has its own version of a sex offender registry, but California was the first to create one in 1947. In the state, those who have committed such crimes as possession of child pornography, sexual battery, child molestation, rape or indecent exposure are required to register their whereabouts with local law enforcement agencies, after their release from prison, jail, probation, parole or a mental hospital. Most offenders must tell law enforcement where they're living annually, but based on the severity of their crimes, some are required to do so every 90 days. Some 63,000 of the state's registrants are displayed on the Megan's Law Web site, including the offenders' photo, address, offenses, scars, marks, tattoos and any known aliases.

Although it's a felony not to keep one's registration up to date, many do not. The National Center for Missing and Exploited Children estimates that of almost 600,000 registered sex offenders in the U.S., there are about 100,000 who legally are required to register their whereabouts but have not done so.

GPS for Offenders Meets with Skepticism

In his TV interview, Runner stressed that wearing a GPS bracelet would not just help law enforcement keep track of sex offenders, it would prevent repeat crimes. "We believe . . . people

129

will behave differently because they know that somebody can check out where they've been," he said. He suggested that wearing an electronic monitoring device for life is not only good for public safety, it's good for the reformed offender, who will be able to prove his alibi every time a new sex crime is committed. "Right now, the normal operating procedure for law enforcement, when there's a sexual attack, is they start knocking on doors of all the people who are registered sex offenders, and they have to prove that they weren't there. The GPS will help them be able to do that."

Slapping a GPS bracelet on someone who is not on probation or parole could be considered seizure.

The critics are not sold. They scoff at the notion that a criminal who will not register voluntarily with the state once a year will keep wearing a GPS ankle bracelet, much less diligently recharge the battery every night. "It's a felony for them not to register, so if they're going to commit a felony, why would they leave their GPS unit on?" says Robert Coombs, director of public affairs for the California Coalition Against Sexual Assault, a statewide coalition of 66 rape crisis centers. "It's really naive to think that this is going to solve the problems." Attorney Stein agrees. "GPS devices can be easily removed," he says. "They're not encased in kryptonite."

The ankle bracelets can be rigged to trigger an alarm with law enforcement if they are cut off. But an offender determined to evade the law could simply let the battery run down. A 2004 study of parolees in Washington state who wore the GPS bracelet found that 6 percent of the devices were lost or damaged by the offenders wearing them. Even the working devices sometimes failed. Satellite technology is not that effective in indoor places like a large mall, building or stadium, or outdoors in a canyonlike environment, like Manhattan. Then there's the question of how already-taxed law enforcement will be deployed to monitor all this data on thousands of people who aren't even on parole. In the Washington study, three of the 42 parolees who wore the device absconded. One homeless offender said his charging stand was stolen.

Will wearing a GPS device make a sex offender less likely to strike again? The research is spotty, simply because no one has been wearing the devices for the decades that the new laws propose. Current studies simply show that the devices may nudge offenders to follow the conditions of their parole. One Florida Department of Corrections study of sex offender parolees found that those who were on electronic monitoring were less likely to have their parole revoked than those who were not being so monitored. Another study of those under house arrest found that they were less likely to violate the terms of their home confinement or abscond than those who were not.

"It looks like electronic monitoring works fine for sex offenders, but it doesn't work any better for them than for any other kind of offenders," says Kathy Padgett, professor in the College of Criminology and Criminal Justice at Florida State University, who conducted the latter study. "It may not have as big an effect because they're less likely to reoffend." Indeed, contrary to popular belief, sex offenders are significantly less likely than other criminals to be rearrested, according to the U.S. Department of Justice's Bureau of Justice Statistics.

Robert Jacob Goldenflame, who goes by Jake Goldenflame, is one of California's registered sex offenders, a convicted child molester, who has now been out of prison for almost 16 years. Goldenflame, who describes himself as in "recovery," is a proponent of the sex offender registry because he believes it helps provide community oversight that makes offenders like himself less likely to strike again. "There is no recovery without registration," he is fond of saying. While making media appearances from Oprah to MSNBC. Goldenflame, who runs a Web site that provides a forum for registered sex offenders and their friends and family, argues that there is no cure for sex offenders like him, but he believes that their risk of committing another crime can be greatly reduced, as it has in his own case. Yet he doesn't think that broadly applying GPS will help the cause.

When he was first out of prison on parole, Goldenflame says, by way of example—a shocking one—he was living in a rooming house run by a Buddhist organization. One of his chores was to take care of two watchdogs in the backyard. Neighborhood kids would walk by and see him with the dogs. One day, one of them, a 12-year-old boy, knocked on the door of his room, and Goldenflame, not knowing who was there, told him to come in. Nothing happened, but Goldenflame points out that if something had, the GPS wouldn't have sounded the alarm that he'd violated the conditions of his parole by being alone with the boy. The device would have shown him where he was supposed to be, in his own room in the rooming house.

"If I raped the child, it wouldn't have told you that. It just tells where I am, but not what I am doing," he says. "I think that this use of GPS promotes a false sense of security. I think that many people may not be thinking it through. They may be thinking it's some kind of camera or Big Brother eye. It does nothing of the sort."

Legal and Civil Rights Challenges Posed by GPS Monitoring

In passive mode, the GPS receiver logs its position relative to satellites at set intervals, storing that information in memory on the device for later retrieval. For instance, an offender could use a land-line phone to download the information once a day to authorities. In "active" mode, which is naturally more expensive to operate, that same info would be sent through a cellphone to law enforcement for real-time monitoring of higher-risk offenders. The state of Florida [as of

2006] spends $10 per day per offender, or about $3,650 a year, for active monitoring. If California outfits felony sex offenders with GPS monitors, costs would run in the tens of millions, growing to $100 million annually in as little as 10 years, reports the state's Legislative Analyst's Office.

Being forced to wear the device while in the privacy of one's home could . . . be considered a search.

The California law, however, is not set in stone. A San Francisco judge has already imposed a preliminary injunction on the residency portions of the law, pending a lawsuit by a sex offender. The GPS portion of the law is currently facing two court challenges. In federal court for the central district of California, a suit charges that such lifetime monitoring is excessive. In federal district court in Sacramento, a sex offender who is currently on parole is suing, arguing that he should not have to wear a GPS monitor for life because it amounts to a new punishment, meted out after the fact.

Jerry Brown, the state's newly elected attorney general, who supported Proposition 83, has said he will not comment on how his office will interpret the law until he takes office early [in 2007]. So it's unclear if the state will attempt to apply the new restrictions to currently registered sex offenders, or merely impose them going forward on offenders who commit crimes after Nov. 7, 2006. But one thing is clear: Jerry Brown is a fan of GPS. As mayor of Oakland, which is plagued by gang violence, Brown launched a pilot program to track the city's most violent repeat offenders, outfitting 17 of them so far with GPS devices. He's lauded it as a way to provide backup for overtaxed police departments.

If the state should decide to impose the device on all felony sex offenders, whose crimes were committed before the proposition passed, it could run into serious constitutional problems, according to Michael Risher, an attorney with the American Civil Liberties Union of Northern California. The ex post facto clause in both the U.S. and state constitutions means that the government cannot impose a greater punishment for a crime than was allowed when that crime was committed. "You cannot pass a law that increases the punishment for past acts," Risher explains.

To impose GPS retroactively, the state would have to argue that the device is not a form of punishment. Which is the argument made by Allen of the National Center for Missing and Exploited Children. "It's not a penalty," he says. "It's regulation. If people are already obligated to register, this is just improving the means of ensuring compliance with registration."

---

90 percent of child victims know their attacker. And almost half the time that person is a family member.

Offenders may also be able to argue that being constantly monitored on GPS also violates their Fourth Amendment right, not to be subject to unreasonable search and seizure. Slapping a GPS bracelet on someone who is not on probation or parole could be considered seizure. "The government simply has no authority to take somebody off the street, who has already paid his debt to society, served his time, and force him to wear a tracking bracelet," says Risher. "It's giving them a life sentence." Being forced to wear the device while in the privacy of one's home could also be considered a search.

GPS Fails to Protect Children from People They Know

Critics say that beyond the legal issues, the draconian new laws, and in particular the GPS ankle bracelets, will have little impact on preventing crimes against children, who are the victims of most sex crimes. Two-thirds of the victims of sex crimes are under age 18, and 58 percent of those underage victims were under age 12, according to the Department of

Justice. Yet the majority of those victims aren't preyed on by strangers but know their attacker.

Pamela D. Schultz, a survivor of childhood sexual abuse, is skeptical that broad application of GPS technology will do anything to prevent crimes like the one she suffered as a girl, which was committed by a neighbor. Now an associate professor of communications at Alfred University, a private school in western New York, she is the author of *Not Monsters: Analyzing the Stories of Child Molesters*. Schultz is also a mother of two, who has a daughter in the second grade and a 21-month-old son. Regarding the new California laws, she says, "I think it's another example of feel-good legislation to get communities to feel that actual action is being taken to stem the problem. GPS monitoring and residency requirements are not going to do anything with the vast majority of offenders. They're just not."

As the state of California's own sex offender registry Web site attests, 90 percent of child victims know their attacker. And almost half the time that person is a family member. "The vast majority of offenders abuse kids who they know," says Schultz. "They have close relationships with the children and the children's families."

Niki Delson, a social worker who is the spokesperson for the California Coalition on Sexual Offending, which opposed the California proposition, says that GPS monitoring will serve no purpose in most of these cases. "The problem with using GPS for people who committed incest is you can't establish a zone which would make a child safe," says Delson. In fact, many sex offenders continue to be acquainted with their actual victims after the crimes occurred, according to Coombs of the California Coalition Against Sexual Assault. "That person doesn't stop being a father or a brother, and in many cases, is brought back to the family. GPS doesn't fix that," he says.

In fact, many sex crimes, notably those committed by family members or acquaintances, go unreported. Schultz fears that residency requirements and GPS tracking will have the unintended consequence of making victims of these crimes less likely to turn an attacker over to authorities. "When the bulk of abuse happens within families and close relationships, there is going to be less of a tendency to report those crimes," she says. "If something happens inside your family, and you report that, it's going to be plastered all over the place. Not only is the offender under public scrutiny, so are the families of the victims." For these types of offenses, adding GPS monitoring and strict residency requirements into the mix adds "another level of pressure into silence."

Schultz would rather see the tens of millions of dollars California is about to spend monitoring felony sex offenders be poured into counseling for victims of sex crimes and into programs for offenders that aim to prevent recidivism. "As a society we need to become less hysterical and more informed about sexual abuse," she says in an e-mail. "When we demonize the offenders, we're pretty much feeding the crime. We further isolate and alienate the offenders, which is a precipitating factor in many offenders' impulses to act out. We're so focused on the minority of offenders who seem to fit our skewed perceptions of what sexual abuse and sexual abusers should be, we fail to recognize that the crime actually occurs closer to home."

Juveniles Engaging in Consensual Oral Sex Should Not Be Punished

Karen Houppert

Karen Houppert is a New York journalist and contributor to The Nation.

June 12, 2007 was one of those days when, having read the paper you are quite certain it is full of misprints and mistakes—either that or you've slipped down Alice's rabbit hole into a logic-free world.

Are young people in this country really serving 10-year prison sentences for consensual oral sex?

I'm referring, of course, to the highly-publicized case of Genarlow Wilson who is in his second year of prison in Georgia for having received oral sex at a high school New Year's Eve party from a 15-year-old girl when he was 17. While it is true that drugs and alcohol were being used. (What?! You're kidding! At a high school party!?) It is also true that the girl never contended that it was anything but consensual.

Four others at the 2003 party, which was videotaped, pled guilty in order to serve less time. But in the 2005 trial, Wilson stated that he did not want to enter a guilty plea and spend his life registered as a sex offender—precluding him from living in the same home as his 8-year-old sister, among other things—and successfully fought a sexual assault charge. But he was found guilty of aggravated child molestation for the oral sex. This carried a 10-year-minimum sentence in Georgia.

The Georgia law originally included an exception. Dubbed "The Romeo & Juliet" clause, it clarified that teens who engaged in consensual intercourse would be excluded from the 10-year-minimum sentencing requirement. Instead, these offenders would be guilty of a lesser misdemeanor charge. But they forgot to include language about oral sex.

In 2006, state legislators amended the law so that teens engaging in intercourse and/or oral sex could only be charged with a misdemeanor—and serve up to 12 months in jail for the "crime."

When I read about this case, I have an evil fantasy.

I envision a slew of creative activists spreading out across the state of Georgia—with a special emphasis on the home districts of this law's proponents and hey, maybe even the lawmakers' own teens—and collecting the tens (no, wait a minute) hundreds (no wait a minute) thousands (no, wait a minute) tens of thousands (no, wait a minute) hundreds of thousands of teens who have broken the law by having oral sex or intercourse in their "tender years" and flooding the courts with their cases. (Remember, according to the Centers for Disease Control, 70 percent of teens are sexually active by the time they reach 19; the average age of first intercourse is 17; 59 percent of sexually experienced female teens had first sex with a partner who was 1 to 3 years their senior; 13 percent of all 15-year-olds have had intercourse.) I would like to see all these cases stacked on the desk of the over-eager district attorney who has so vigorously pursued this absurd case. And I would like to see state legislators buckling under the cost of these investigations, trials, and long prison sentences.

Some residents in the state have worried that African-American Genarlow Wilson was selectively prosecuted because of his race. I believe the state of Georgia would do well to allay these concerns by pursuing, in a fair and equitable manner, each and every case involving sex among consenting minors. After all, it's a crime, right?

Or have I fallen down some rabbit hole?

Legislation Must Be Based on Scientific Research

Richard B. Krueger

Richard B. Krueger is a psychiatrist and a professor of psychiatry at the College of Physicians and Surgeons, Columbia University.

Increasingly, legislation dealing with sex offenders is being passed that is punitive, untested, expensive and, in many cases, counterproductive—demonizing people who commit sexual offenses without offering any empirical information that the new laws will reduce sexually violent crime.

[In early March 2007,] for instance, New York became the 19th state to enact so-called sexually violent predator legislation. This legislation provides for the indefinite "civil commitment" of sexual offenders who have served their time in prison and are about to be released.

The legislation was passed despite a lack of evidence that such laws actually reduce sexual violence and despite recent reports of warehousing and chaos in some programs and relentlessly rising costs in others.

It is just one example of the kind of punitive laws being passed across the country. Other measures include increasingly strict residency restrictions (such as those imposed by Proposition 83 in California, approved by the voters in November), more stringent rules for community notification regarding sexual offenders and monitoring by GPS [global positioning system] (also mandated under Proposition 83, with cost projections of $100 million annually, according to the state's legislative analyst).

In many states, politicians are eager to pass such legislation, which is enthusiastically supported by the public. Indeed, ask citizens what they think and you're likely to hear that they support laws to "get rid of perverts" who, in the eyes of many people, "deserve what they get."

These days, the pendulum continues to swing further toward the punitive end of the spectrum, with ever more draconian sentencing and post-release conditions.

Changes in Public Opinion and Practice

This is not new. In general, dispassionate discussion of sexuality is difficult, even more so when it comes to sexual crimes. Ebbs and flows of public attention and vilification have often occurred in this country.

In the 1930s and '40s, castration was practiced in California, where sex offenders and homosexuals received this "treatment." Also, the first generation of sexual psychopath laws was passed during this time mandating indefinite commitment for sexually violent predators. In the 1980s, society was roiled by a series of high-profile day-care-center abuse cases (such as the McMartin case and others that proved later to be unfounded). In the 1990s, there was a media uproar over supposed "ritualistic" and "satanic" sexual abuse.

These days, the pendulum continues to swing further toward the punitive end of the spectrum, with ever more draconian sentencing and post-release conditions. Under the federal Adam Walsh Child Protection Act, signed into law by President Bush in July, all sex offenders will be listed on the Internet, making information on offenders, regardless of whether they belong to a low-, medium- or high-risk category, publicly accessible; this includes people, for example, whose only crime is the possession of child pornography.

Obviously, this makes it increasingly difficult for ex-offenders to obtain residences or jobs—the mainstays of stability—and it subjects them to ongoing vigilantism and public censure. Although notification may make sense for some, it does not make sense for all.

In California, the most recent debate has been over whether Proposition 83, the law passed [in 2006] banning registered sex offenders from living within 2,000 feet of a school or park, can be retroactively applied to the 90,000 offenders who have already been released from prison. (Two federal judges ruled last month that it may not.)

Demonizing Offenders Decreases Public Safety

What is being created is a class of individuals that is progressively demonized by society and treated in such a way that a meaningful reintegration into society is impossible.

The current public discourse on sex offenders is . . . without a base of empirical studies.

Yes, sexual abuse is a serious matter. Yes, individuals who commit sexual crimes should be punished. Unquestionably, a small percentage of sex offenders are very dangerous and must be removed from society. What's more, we know that sexual crimes are devastating to victims and their families and that we must do all we can to protect ourselves from "predators."

But demonizing people rather than treating them makes little sense, and passing laws that are tough but mindless in response to political pressure won't solve the problem either.

The reality is that, despite the popular perception to the contrary, recidivism rates for sexual offenders are among the lowest of any class of criminals. What's more, 90% of sex offenders in prison will eventually be released back into the community—and 90% of sexual offenses are committed by people known to their victim, such as family members or trusted members of the community—so rehabilitation is critical. It is not possible, affordable, constitutional or reasonable to lock up all sex offenders all of the time.

Society's efforts to segregate sex offenders are backfiring, resulting in unintended consequences. Homelessness is increasing among sex offenders, for instance, making it harder to monitor them and causing some law enforcement officials to call for a repeal of residency restrictions.

One of the greatest challenges to workable civil commitment programs is that offenders are so feared that, when they are ready to be reintroduced into society, no community will accept them—so instead they remain institutionalized indefinitely, creating ever-increasing costs without an end in sight.

Irrational Fears Spawn Irrational Legislation

Why has this demonization occurred? One reason is that offenders are hot news, and the more heinous the sexual crime, the more the media focus on it. Thus, our minds create a stereotype of egregious evil with respect to all sex offenders. We no longer distinguish between the most egregious cases and the others, despite the fact that the most terrible crimes represent only a small proportion of all sexual offenses.

But there *are* less serious crimes, and we should acknowledge that. Possession of child pornography is categorically different from a sexual assault. So is exhibitionism. The wife of a man who committed a hands-off crime involving possession of child pornography put it this way: "Each of these horrendous crimes drives another nail into our coffin."

Another reason for the demonization is that society has failed to fund research on the treatment and management of people convicted of sexual crimes—despite the fact that states are willing to spend hundreds of millions of dollars on unproven programs for treatment and containment.

The current public discourse on sex offenders is, therefore, without a base of empirical studies. Psychiatry, psychology and our national research institutes have eschewed involvement with such research.

No one is suggesting that sexual crimes should go unpunished or that some of the newer approaches—such as medication, intensive community supervision or even carefully considered civil commitment—are without value. What is becoming clearer, however, is that the climate in the United States makes reasonable discussion difficult.

What can be done? Some scholars, in an effort to interpose rationality between public fear and legislation, have suggested the concept of "evidence-based legislation." This is analogous to "evidence-based medicine" and would call on legislative bodies to inform their proposed laws with the best available scientific evidence—something that is rarely done now.

What is happening now with individuals who have committed sexual crimes is the modern-day equivalent of a witch hunt. Our images of the worst determine what we mete out to all sex offenders. It is time to reexamine our approaches and develop empirically based, scientifically sound measures and treatments to bring rationality back to this discussion.

Death Penalty for Sex Offenders Sends the Wrong Message

Debra Saunders

Debra Saunders is a columnist for the San Francisco Chronicle.

Oklahoma's governor, Brad Henry, a Democrat, signed a bill [in June 2006] that would allow jurors to sentence to death repeat sex offenders for crimes against children younger than 14. The day before, South Carolina Gov. Mark Sanford, a Republican, signed a bill that would allow capital punishment for repeat offenders guilty of sex crimes against children younger than 11. Sanford announced that the bill would be "an incredibly powerful deterrent to offenders that have been released."

I could not disagree more—and I support the death penalty, and believe that men (and women) who repeatedly rape or molest children deserve harsh punishment and long, hard time in the big house.

It is a fine principle of American jurisprudence that the state does not mete out a punishment greater than the crime.

Michael Rushford of the pro-death penalty Criminal Justice Legal Foundation in Sacramento, Calif., captured my thoughts exactly when he said: "It's like this. If you get a death sentence for raping a little girl, and you get a death sentence for raping a little girl and killing a little girl, and the only witness to the crime is the little girl, why not kill them all?"

The Death Penalty for Non-Capital Crimes Is Unconstitutional

These bills are likely to eat up a lot of tax dollars on appeals—then lose, as the U.S. Supreme Court seems predisposed to overturn the new legislation.

Since the U.S. Supreme Court reinstated the death penalty in 1976, no one has been executed in America for a crime that did not involve murder. In 1977, the court ruled that it was unconstitutional to execute a man for the crime of raping an adult woman—and this rape occurred as the rapist escaped from a Georgia prison, where he was serving time for murder, rape, kidnapping and aggravated assault.

The Big Bench ruled that "a sentence of death is grossly disproportionate and excessive punishment for the crime of rape and is therefore forbidden by the Eighth Amendment as cruel and unusual punishment." It is a fine principle of American jurisprudence that the state does not mete out a punishment greater than the crime.

Since 1976, five states have passed laws to allow execution for sex crimes against children, but according to The Associated Press, only one inmate has been sentenced to death—he raped an 8-year-old girl in Louisiana—and his case is pending on appeal.

Rushford noted the many judges who would oppose the death penalty, even for an unrepentant multiple murderer like Stanley "Tookie" Williams, who was executed in December. Ergo, even more judges will look at the death penalty for sex offenders and "are going to step up to say, 'This is over the line.'"

And: "If I were an opponent of the death penalty, I would probably support the Oklahoma law." I called Lance Lindsey of Death Penalty Focus, which opposes capital punishment. Lindsey told me he opposes the law, too: "Essentially, I'm against the government killing prisoners."

Here are two additional reasons other states should not follow Oklahoma. First, the hint of child abuse can spawn a witch-hunt atmosphere in the courts. Authorities have been known to coax young children to accuse innocent adults, and prosecutors have charged child-care providers based on testimony that was hard to believe when cooler heads prevailed. Witness the infamous McMartin preschool case in 1983.

Second. America's laws should not send a message that the victims of sexual assaults have been harmed irrevocably, as murder victims are. No victim survives murder. Rape presents horrific trauma—however, over time, most victims, even child victims, can overcome the pain and sense of violation. I don't want laws that tell child victims they have experienced something as damaging as murder. They've been hurt enough.

Castration Should Be an Option for Sex Offenders

Tamara Dietrich

Tamara Dietrich is a columnist for the Daily Press, *Newport News, Virginia.*

They say that when somebody reveals something unflattering about himself, believe it.

Maybe he drinks too much, or he's afraid to commit. Maybe he's a moody sort.

Whatever it is, don't pooh-pooh the confession or figure the poor guy is being too hard on himself.

Believe it, believe it, believe it.

And if a guy tells you he can't stop thinking about having sex with little girls and the only cure is castration, for goodness sake, hand him a straight razor.

The problem with conflicted pedophile James Jenkins is, nobody took him at his word.

Jenkins freely admitted his brain was filled with deviant sexual fantasies of young girls. He insisted he needed to be neutered.

But unlike eight other states, Virginia doesn't yet allow high-risk sex offenders to opt for castration—chemical or surgical.

So three years ago in an Accomack County jail cell, Jenkins bit the plastic casing off a shaving razor, tied off his scrotum with shoelaces, bit into an apple to stifle his screams and went from rooster to hen faster than you can sing "Do You Really Want to Hurt Me."

Tamara Dietrich, "State Should Reconsider Castration for Predators," *Daily Press*, Newport News, Va., August 9, 2006. Copyright © 2006 *Daily Press*, Newport News, Va. Reproduced by permission.

"I was convinced that was the only salvation for me," Jenkins is quoted as saying in Sunday [August 6, 2006]'s *Daily Press*, "I had to think about my testicles versus life in prison."

Frankly, I would have mustered more sympathy for the guy if his concerns had tended more toward his young victims, past and future, and less toward his own body parts and where they might be spending the next 30 years.

Think of the lives and futures we could save with human spay-and-neuter clinics and the right client list.

Castration Should Be Broadly Applied to Criminals

Virginia lawmakers had the chance [in 2006] to allow high-risk sex offenders like Jenkins to volunteer for surgical castration at the hands of professionals, but they passed on the idea.

Instead, taxpayers are building a $62 million facility to warehouse, we hope, the worst of the worst in civil confinement once their criminal sentences are up.

At least it's a plan.

We can debate ad nauseum the merits of castration versus confinement, chemicals versus scalpels, whether rape is a crime of lust or a crime of power and domination, whether castration is a civilized option or even an effective one, and the many ways in which a castrated male can still sexually violate a victim.

What I'd rather discuss is how to take the castration idea and really run with it.

Why stop with males who sexually violate children? Why not include males who murder children?

And, for that matter, why not include females who maim or murder children?

I bet we can all name miscreants of both genders who should never, ever be allowed in the proximity of minors: homicidal parents, abusive live-ins, psychotic babysitters.

Think of the lives and futures we could save with human spay-and-neuter clinics and the right client list.

Mothers like Tammy Skinner of Suffolk, who admitted shooting her own baby out of her belly. Live-ins like Misty Fuller of Isle of Wight, charged with bashing in the head of her boyfriend's toddler.

Daddies like Elijah Tyrone Mitchell of Hampton, convicted last month in the beating death of his 8-week-old baby daughter. Babysitters like Shane Joseph Cartwright of Williamsburg, charged in June with abuse and neglect after the 1-year-old boy in his charge had his skull fractured.

Crimes like this don't generally call for natural life in prison. Crimes like this, you do your time and you're out again.

And all bets are off.

We're Too Lenient with Criminals

Sure, the notion of human spay-and-neuter clinics will never merit serious consideration in the mainstream. At least, not as a punishment or deterrent for violent criminal behavior against women and children.

We're not that kind of people.

Instead, we're the kind of people who spend millions in taxpayer dollars to confine and try to "reform" people like Jenkins, who tell us point blank that we're deluding ourselves. Jenkins supports the castration bill.

We're the kind of people that dump too many sexually violent predators back into the community after they've paid their dues, manhood intact.

We're the kind of people who are unmoved by European studies showing a recidivism rate of only 3 percent to 7 percent among sex offenders who underwent chemical or surgical castration. Studies showing that, of those not castrated, 39 percent to 52 percent reoffended.

[In 2007,] Virginia lawmakers will have a chance to consider the castration bill again.

[In 2007,] let's see if they finally have the apples for it.

Castration Is Inappropriate and Immoral

Daily Press, Newport News, Virginia

The editorial board of the Daily Press *provided their opinion on the matter of castration for sexual offenders after posing the question for readers' comments.*

How did such a quease-inducing topic as castration become part of a national debate?

By way of the frenzy of public attention focused on sexual predators, a frenzy inflamed by a few, high-profile cases involving children, by widening recognition of the threat posed by the Internet as a way for offenders to find victims, by a barrage of newspaper stories and cable news specials.

Outrage at the prevalence of sexual crimes leads immediately to the question: What's the best way to punish offenders and prevent them from claiming more victims? One option, presented by some offenders and some legislators, is castration.

It is controversial. There is debate over whether castration is effective, whether it is humane, whether it is something the government should be involved in.

[The week of August 6, 2006,] we asked readers to join in the debate. We heard from eight. What does that mean? That people aren't concerned about the problem, or that they don't have strong opinions on the matter, or they don't know what to think?

Those who have made up their minds, and shared them with us, were split. Three thought sex offenders (or child molesters) should be castrated, and one, a victim of childhood abuse, thought it far too merciful. Two cautioned that it may not be an effective or appropriate solution. A couple offered up judges and politicians as recipients of the procedure.

Sex Offenders Should Not Be Castrated

The Editorial Board joins the naysayers, with the opinion that the state should not castrate sex offenders. Here's our reasoning:

When imposed by the state, castration seems a barbaric enterprise for the government to be engaged in.

When it is offered as an alternative to long-term confinement—as is the case under a proposal in Virginia—it's a dicey proposition. The issue here is the offenders who scare everyone the most: those likely to reoffend. A few, horrific cases spurred Virginia to put in place a new program to screen sex offenders nearing release to assess whether they will continue to be a danger. It developed a mechanism to keep the high-risk ones off the streets: civil commitment, a procedure in which courts can order people with psychiatric problems who pose a danger to themselves, or others, to be confined in mental health settings. Virginia's facility for committed sex offenders both treats them and keeps them away from the public—indefinitely. This year, Sen. Emmett Hanger introduced a bill that would allow offenders the choice of surgical castration rather than commitment; a committee put it off till next year.

There's a problem with castration as an option to commitment: It would put these individuals back on the street rather than tucking them away. Given the unresolved questions about how well castration works, this doesn't afford society enough protection.

Sexual crime can arise from origins other than sexual desire: from issues related to anger or control or domination or self-image, from deep-seated feelings about women, from childhood experience. Disrupting the flow of hormones by way of castration won't deal with these drivers.

And castration can be undone. Testosterone supplements aren't hard to come by.

When imposed by the state, castration seems a barbaric enterprise for the government to be engaged in. The effects can harm the body inflicting that punishment, as well as the individuals on whom it is inflicted. Do the people really want mutilation to be done in their name? Do we want to be that kind of society? The answer should be no. That's why legislative proposals, like that advanced by Del. Tom Gear a couple of years ago, that would mandate chemical castration of a wide range of offenders are the wrong choice.

Castration can appeal for a couple of reasons. There's an undeniable desire for vengeance when we consider the victims of sexual abuse, particularly children. There are offenders who want it.

But between questions about its efficacy and questions about its morality, it is not a choice the state should make.

And consider this: The vast majority of children who are sexually abused—and tens of thousands are, each year, in Virginia—aren't the victims of prior sex offenders. They're the victims of fathers, grandfathers, uncles, ministers, coaches, teachers, family friends and, for teenagers, dates. Our efforts are better spent preventing, detecting and responding to this threat, the one we don't like to face.

CHAPTER 4

How Can Sex Offender Policies Be Improved?

Chapter Preface

While many experts agree that sex offenders' crimes, particularly those committed against children, call for increased vigilance in managing known offenders, they caution that management strategies that rely too heavily upon punishment and public shaming of sex offenders may backfire, and increase the likelihood that a sex offender will commit further crimes. Research and practical experience has demonstrated the effectiveness of managing and monitoring sex offenders, which helps them take responsibility for their actions and supports them in their efforts to reform their lives. Such an approach does not preclude registration, tracking, or community notification for some offenders. In addition, experts assert, since the vast majority of children are sexually victimized by family members and acquaintances who have no criminal record, the best approach to reducing child sex abuse focuses on community education about how offenders gain through "grooming," and on helping parents identify pedophiles before they have an opportunity to commit crimes.

The harshest penalties, experts argue, should be reserved for the small percentage of offenders who are truly predatory and highly likely to commit numerous sexual assaults. Other experts maintain that harsher penalties and clear policies need to be put into place to deal with child pornographers, and for pedophiles who use the Internet to solicit sex with minors. These experts warn that the Internet is a powerful weapon for sexual predators, and call for a collaboration between business, technology, government, and law enforcement to devise a strategy to disarm predators and safeguard children.

In its April 2002 guide to effective sex offender management, the Center for Sex Offender Management (CSOM), a program within the U.S. Department of Justice, summed up the views of many experts regarding the best course of action to improve sex offender policy. The report stated:

> Current interventions directed to ending sexual abuse focus primarily on intervening with offenders who have already perpetrated sex offenses. However, criminal justice system actors who envision a response to sexual violence beyond the bounds of their own system must begin to forge collaborative partnerships with those in the public health and primary prevention arenas in an effort to stop sexual violence before it occurs. Recognition that sexual assault is a public health problem is steadily gaining momentum and a body of literature and research regarding its prevention is emerging.

Policy Should Emphasize Public Health and Restorative Justice

Eric S. Janus

Eric S. Janus is vice dean and professor of law at William Mitchell College of Law. He is the author of Failure to Protect: America's Sexual Predator Laws and the Rise of the Preventive State, *from which this excerpt is taken.*

The predator laws represent an approach to sexual violence that is out of balance. The great bulk of sexual victimization is perpetrated by men who have not been in the criminal justice system and who are acquaintances and even intimates of the victims. Sexual predator commitment laws confine only a small percentage of the sex offenders who are under correctional control, releasing a large majority of recidivists back into the community. Yet the predator commitment laws are exceedingly expensive and growing, while programs that address a broader swath of violence must struggle for funding. If we simply consider the number of sexual victimizations addressed, the cost of sex predator commitment laws seems grossly out of proportion.

We must reexamine the predator model and the resource allocation it entails, broadening the question we ask when designing sexual violence policy. The predator model focuses on the "worst of the worst" and seeks to identify and lock up the "most dangerous." Instead, we should be asking what combination of approaches to sexual violence has the best prospect of preventing the most sexual violence. This entails a shift from focusing mainly on assessing individual risk to under-

Eric S. Janus, "There Are Alternatives," *Failure to Protect: America's Sexual Predator Laws and the Rise of the Preventive State*, Ithaca, NY: Cornell University Press, 2006. Copyright © 2006 by Cornell University. Used by permission of the publisher, Cornell University Press.

standing and addressing risk both individually and collectively, from addressing mainly the most obvious and visible dangers to attempting to prevent the hidden and silent crimes that make up the bulk of sexual victimization. . . .

The Public Health Approach

Many of the most thoughtful commentators on the prevention of sexual violence urge a public health approach to the problem of sexual violence. Sexual violence, like the classic infectious diseases (smallpox, measles, polio), has widespread negative effects on our society. The public health approach, a systematic application of scientific learning aimed at understanding and addressing root causes, could help effectively reduce sexual violence in the same way that it has controlled many infectious diseases.

The predator laws exemplify an approach that is 180 degrees from these public health principles.

The public health approach entails a systematic method of analysis, a way of seeing the problem in a larger, more contextualized framework. It divides interventions into three categories: primary, secondary, and tertiary. Primary prevention efforts focus on stopping sexually abusive behaviors before they start. They aim at changing the conditions that produce the problem—attacking the root causes of sexual violence. Secondary programs focus on "those at high risk for offending as well as stopping recent sexual offenders from re-offending." Tertiary prevention "involves trying to stop future violence by those who have a history of offending behaviors."

The public health approach uses systematic and empirically based information for deciding how best to attack a public health problem like sexual violence. It consciously looks beyond individual characteristics of offenders to identify causes that exist at a societal or community level. These classic steps that enabled public health to conquer infectious disease aim to address sexual violence comprehensively. The first step is "ongoing systematic collection, analysis, and interpretation of data on the incidence, prevalence, and risk factors." The second step is "identifying causes" through research. The third step is the "development and evaluation of programs." Finally, the public health model engages in "dissemination and implementation . . . communicating which preventive programs work based on evaluation of data and putting these programs into practice."

The public health approach helps us understand the difference between thinking about a problem like sexual violence at the scale of individuals and thinking about it from the perspective of the population as a whole. The public health approach allows us to see that there is collective risk as well as individual risk, and that the worst of the worst account for only a fraction of the collective risk posed by sexual violence. The public health approach, by insisting on empirically based policies for reducing sexual violence, puts "prevention efforts foremost." Unlike the conventional narrow and politicized approach that values only punishment, public health advocates understand the need for a "comprehensive approach addressing all levels of prevention (i.e., primary, secondary, and tertiary)."

The predator laws exemplify an approach that is 180 degrees from these public health principles. The predator laws were not based on research. They make no pretense of attacking the root causes of sexual violence or changing the conditions that produce it. Rather, they take a simple containment approach to those who are already identified as dangerous offenders. Far from being comprehensive, they focus only on a small part of the problem, a part that is far removed from the root causes or the experiences of most victims of sexual violence. There has been little research about the effectiveness of the predator law approaches and little reason to believe that they have reduced the scope of sexual violence in any meaningful way. Robert Prentky and Ann Burgess are leading scholars of sexual violence and the design of systems for attempting to reduce it. They point out that despite the "hypervigilant" and "draconian" responses to sexual violence, "by and large, those who sexually intimidate and sexually coerce others do so with impunity." Along with many other experts, they urge a model that "treats sexual assault as a public health problem."

Primary Prevention Is Best

The public health approach helps us see what a focus on identified individual offenders hides: the value and necessity of primary prevention. Because most sexual violence does not show up in the criminal justice system, most will remain unaddressed by secondary and tertiary interventions. Primary prevention is proactive, while the secondary and tertiary methods are reactive. Primary prevention aims at addressing sexual violence before it happens. Secondary and tertiary approaches become applicable only after an offender has begun abusing victims.

The primary focus of restorative justice is on redressing harm to the victim.

Although primary prevention programs are in their infancy, and their effectiveness is as yet unproven, they have a number of attractions. They are relatively cheap and can reach large numbers of people. They aim to change root causes of sexual violence by addressing attitudes, beliefs, and behaviors and thus stop sexual violence before it begins. Secondary and tertiary approaches, in contrast, do not address new entrants into sexual offending, but confine their attention to those who have already offended.

Stop It Now! is a grassroots organization founded by Fran Henry, a survivor of childhood sexual abuse. The group advocates a paradigm shift, the creation of "a new pathway for preventing child sexual abuse—a path that uses the powerful tools of public health and prevents abuse before it happens." A recent publication explains:

> While individual cases are extremely important, we now recognize that child sexual abuse is not just the result of individual pathologies and aberrant families; it is a widespread social illness, requiring social action and change, and primary, "front end" prevention strategies.... We need a proactive, prevention-based model that will address the root causes of abuse on a social systems scale: that is what public health can offer.

Another key advocate of public health approaches is Kathleen Basile, an official with the Centers for Disease Control and Prevention. Citing a long list of other authors, Basile states that "more attention should be given to primary prevention of sexual violence if real gains are to be made in decreasing this problem." Basile argues that "national campaigns against sexual violence in the media could affect rates of sexual offending by gradually influencing societal norms that condone sexual aggression." She cites campaigns regarding the use of automobile seat belts, noting that today about two-thirds of the population uses seat belts, "largely because the norms about wearing seat belts have changed through public awareness combined with changes in laws." Smoking cessation campaigns provide another example of the larger society getting involved in preventing a widespread problem. She states that "the same societal urgency needs to be established around decreasing sexual violence perpetration by involving the public in large-scale sexual violence preventive efforts."

Prevention Programs in Development

Primary prevention programs are largely in the developmental stage. Some experimental programs seek to change attitudes and behaviors among school-age populations. Safe Dates, a program offered to middle school students in rural South Carolina, seeks to change norms around dating violence, to decrease gender stereotyping, and to enhance conflict management. The program also offers services for adolescents in abusive relationships. Early research indicates that the program is successful in reducing sexual violence on dates. Another program, in a midsize city in the Pacific Northwest, was designed to challenge high school students' "attitudes about coercive sexual behavior" and teach them "ways to deal with unwanted sexual advances through clear communication." The program was subjected to a controlled evaluation, which indicated that "students with more negative attitudes about sexual assault benefited the most from the program." Other programs, aimed at high-risk adolescent males, report some success at decreasing rape-myth acceptance.

The process seeks to acknowledge the harm but also works with the offender and the community to prevent further harm.

Another approach advocated by Stop It Now! and other groups is to facilitate early intervention where there is a risk of sexual abuse. This involves public education about the signs that sexual deviancy is developing in a child or that an adult is engaging in sexually exploitive or abusive behavior. It also involves helping people know what to do and where to turn to obtain help to stop sexual abuse. Stop It Now! produced a social marketing campaign aimed at abusers and potential abusers. Employing "provocative ads that highlighted the effectiveness of treatment," they "encouraged abusers to stop hurting children, urged offenders to get help, and prompted family members to call for assistance." Evaluation suggested that the program produced "several dramatic changes" in the public's knowledge about child sexual abuse. In addition, the Stop It Now! campaign recognizes and attempts to remove the barriers for abusers seeking help without exposing themselves to unduly harsh consequences of shaming and exclusion. In a pilot program in Vermont, fifteen adults and ten adolescents self-reported their abusive behavior to authorities, and clinicians reported that twenty adults and ninety-eight juveniles voluntarily entered treatment without a direct victim report.

A report commissioned by the Centers for Disease Control discussed very preliminary results from a program to identify and evaluate primary prevention approaches to sexual violence. Preliminary results from the study found some significant increases in participants' knowledge regarding consent and in their intentions to prevent disrespectful behavior, though there were some results in the opposite direction. The report states:

> Participant feedback measures have demonstrated strong positive response to the intervention by youth. Qualitative data from focus groups in three sites indicates that programs are changing participants' concepts of healthy and unhealthy relationships and enhancing their ability to recognize and respond to sexual harassment.

Primary prevention efforts "are essentially at the drawing boards." Pursuing these promising leads will require additional resources for experimentation and careful evaluations, and dissemination and implementation of the approaches that are shown to be most effective. . . .

Restorative Justice

Restorative justice approaches seek to facilitate offender reintegration while emphasizing the importance of accountability and community safety. The restorative justice movement argues that restorative approaches produce greater prospects of safety, because they place offenders within a web of relationships that helps ensure accountability and safe behavior. The primary focus of restorative justice is on redressing harm to the victim. These programs operate at both the internal and external levels, providing "opportunities for hope and recovery" and a feeling of acceptance, along with the kinds of family and community connections that enable the community to exert its normal forms of control. The key is the ability of these programs to accommodate and promote both "accountability and understanding." According to sociology professor Lois Presser and criminal justice professor Elaine Gunnison, "Restorative justice stresses the need to repair the harms caused by crime and to reintegrate victims, offenders, and communities."

Mary Koss, Karen Bachar, and C. Quince Hopkins run a program called RESTORE (Responsibility and Equity for Sexual Transgressions Offering a Restorative Experience) in Pima County, Arizona. The program deals with date and acquaintance rape and nonpenetration sexual offenses. The RESTORE program "emphasizes offender accountability through reparations and rehabilitation rather than punishment and aims to transform the community's role in addressing crime." RESTORE is a victim-centered diversion program, offering victims the option of addressing the sexual violence through a process that consciously is designed to eliminate the kinds of trauma associated with the formal systems of criminal adjudication.

This program uses a restorative justice technique called community conferencing that brings together "victims, offenders, and their supporters for a face-to-face meeting in the presence of a facilitator." At this conference, the participants "discuss the effects of the incident on them" and "make a plan to repair the damage done and minimize the likelihood of further harm." The aim is to have the offender accept responsibility, make things right, and earn redemption. Similar restorative programs, most of which address programs for juvenile offenders, have high success rates: 90 percent of restitution agreements made in restorative programs are completed within a year, compared with 20–30 percent compliance in more typical court-ordered restitution programs.

Another example of restorative justice is the Canadian Circles of Support and Accountability, operated by the Mennonite Church and supported by a small grant from the Correctional Service of Canada, discussed at some length in Jon Silverman and David Wilson's book about responses to pedophilia, *Innocence Betrayed*. Working with offenders as they are released from prison, six people form a virtual circle around the offender in the community. The members of the circle visit the "core member" each day, "both to support [the offender] and hold him accountable for his attitudes and actions within the community." The circles are not treatment. Rather, they provide support and accountability. The process seeks to acknowledge the harm but also works with the offender and the community to prevent further harm. The "intended result is to reduce reoffending through deterrence and prevention, rather than relying on punishment." The approach has gotten support not only from the Canadian Correctional Service but also from Toronto's Sexual Abuse Squad. In their description of the project, Silverman and Wilson quote an officer on the squad, Detective Constable Brian Thomson, whom they call "as traditional a 'cop' as you could ever hope to find." Thomson finds the circles indispensable in supervising sex offenders in the community. Eileen Henderson, a "typical Canadian 'soccer mum'" who coordinates the Circles, posits that it is the idea of community that is at the heart of the Circles' success. "I think it's about people forming a community, and not excluding anyone. Looking at everyone as people." Said one of the volunteers: "The bottom line is that these people are not monsters sent from another planet. They came out of our communities and we have to find ways of working with them in the community while at the same time keeping that community safe." Silverman and Wilson characterize the Circles as "controlling through inclusion."

Policy Shift Needed to Protect Children on the Internet

Michelle Collins

Michelle Collins is the director of the Exploited Child Unit for the National Center for Missing & Exploited Children. She testified before the U.S. House of Representatives Committee on Energy and Commerce's subcommittee on telecommunications and the Internet regarding the research conducted on child victimization via the Internet.

Mr. Chairman and distinguished members of the [U.S. House of Representatives Committee on Energy and Commerce]. I welcome this opportunity to appear before you to discuss social networking websites and the use of the Internet to victimize children. Chairman [Fred] Upton, you have a demonstrated record of commitment to child protection and I commend you and your colleagues for your leadership and initiative. The National Center for Missing & Exploited Children ("NCMEC") joins you in your concern for the safety of the most vulnerable members of our society and thanks you for bringing attention to this serious problem facing America's communities.

Let me first provide you with some background information about the National Center for Missing & Exploited Children (NCMEC). NCMEC is a not-for-profit corporation, mandated by Congress and working in partnership with the U.S. Department of Justice as the national resource center and clearinghouse on missing and exploited children. NCMEC is a true public-private partnership, funded in part by Congress and in part by the private sector. Our federal funding supports specific operational functions mandated by Congress,

Michelle Collins, testimony given before the U.S. House of Representatives Committee on Energy and Commerce's Subcommittee on Telecommunications and the Internet, www.missingkids.com, July 11, 2006. Reproduced by permission of the author.

including a national 24-hour toll-free hotline; a distribution system for missing-child photos; a system of case management and technical assistance to law enforcement and families; training programs for federal, state and local law enforcement; and our programs designed to help stop the sexual exploitation of children.

Programs to Fight Internet Crimes Against Children

These programs include the CyberTipline, the "9-1-1 for the Internet," which serves as the national clearinghouse for investigative leads and tips regarding crimes against children on the Internet. The Internet has become a primary tool to victimize children today, due to its widespread use and the relative anonymity that it offers child predators. Our CyberTipline is operated in partnership with the Federal Bureau of Investigation ("FBI"), the Department of Homeland Security's Bureau of Immigration and Customs Enforcement ("ICE"), the U.S Postal Inspection Service, the U.S. Secret Service, the U.S. Department of Justice's Child Exploitation and Obscenity Section and the Internet Crimes Against Children Task Forces, as well as state and local law enforcement. Leads are received in seven categories of crimes:

- possession, manufacture and distribution of child pornography;
- online enticement of children for sexual acts;
- child prostitution;
- child-sex tourism;
- child sexual molestation (not in the family);
- unsolicited obscene material sent to a child; and
- misleading domain names.

This last category was added as a result of enactment of the PROTECT Act in 2003.

The Internet has provided a veil of apparent anonymity, enabling predators to seek out children, win their confidence and then victimize them.

These leads are reviewed by NCMEC analysts, who visit the reported sites, examine and evaluate the content, use search tools to try to identify perpetrators, and provide all lead information to the appropriate law enforcement agency. The FBI, ICE and Postal Inspection Service have "real time" access to the leads, and all three agencies assign agents and analysts to work directly out of NCMEC and review the reports. The results: in the 8 years since the CyberTipline began operation, NCMEC has received and processed more than 400,000 leads, resulting in hundreds of arrests and successful prosecutions.

However, despite our progress the victimization of children continues and there is evidence that it is increasing. The number of reports of online enticement of children to the CyberTipline increased 400 percent since 1998. Our records show a significant and steady increase in these reports over the years. This upward trend is very disturbing and shows the seriousness of this issue. But this is not the only evidence.

It has been established that youth who use the Internet regularly receive sexual solicitations over the Internet. However, very few of these sexual solicitations are reported to authorities. This clearly demonstrates that children are at risk and that we must do more.

Technology Advances Have Led to Criminal Advances

Over the years as technology has evolved so, too, have the methods for victimizing children. The Internet has provided a veil of apparent anonymity, enabling predators to seek out children, win their confidence and then victimize them.

As technology evolves, so does the creativity of the predator. Today, we are hearing a great deal about new innovations, including the use of webcams, social networking websites and Internet access on cell phones.

The unprecedented amount of personal information that teens are posting to social networking websites makes them vulnerable to people who want to harm them.

These innovations are popular and are utilized by millions of Americans. Yet, as with every other new program or service, there are those who would use them inappropriately and for unlawful purposes.

Recently there has been great attention to the social networking websites. While they are used by adults, kids are enormously attracted to them, and there have been instances in which offenders have taken advantage of the images and information displayed to target kids. The unprecedented amount of personal information that teens are posting to social networking websites makes them vulnerable to people who want to harm them.

Some of the social networking sites link defined communities of registered users, such as students attending a particular college or high school. Others are open to anyone over a certain age. These websites permit registered users to create an online profile, including photographs, with categories of interest such as music and sports, as well as an online journal. They are highly personalized and often extremely detailed. Children consider this to be an easy way to connect with friends, find new friends and share their thoughts and feelings. The teenage years are a time of personal explorations. This is only natural. However, the new form of social interaction is over the Internet, exposing children to, literally, a world of potential danger.

Child predators consider these sites to be an easy way to find child victims. They can use the information posted by children to forge a "cyber-relationship" that can lead to that child being victimized. The number of reports to our Cyber-Tipline involving social networking sites has increased. In recent years, many kids were using their email profiles and chat rooms in a similar fashion to share their hobbies and interests and make "friends." However, those forums didn't have nearly the same implications as the social networking sites, with their enormous universe of users.

The industry's brightest minds ... can work together to solve this problem, with the help of policy makers, law enforcement and children's advocacy groups.

Last month [June 2006], NCMEC hosted a Dialogue on Social Networking Sites here in Washington, D.C. It was a day-long series of panelist-audience discussions on the popularity and misuse of this technology and ways to help keep children safer while using them. The panelists included leaders from the technology industry, policy makers, law enforcement, academia and children's advocacy groups. The attendees questioned representatives from the social networking sites Myspace. Facebook, and Xanga, the FBI's Innocent Images Unit, two Internet Crimes Against Children Task Force investigators, age verification and digital imaging analysis experts, the Internet Education Foundation, Net Family News, the Pew Foundation and two state attorneys general.

It was a vigorous and informative exchange.

What did we learn?

Legislation Is Needed to Make the Internet Safer

We learned that social networking sites tap directly into the needs of teenagers to define themselves, explore their own creativity and reach out to their peers. We learned that operators of social networking sites don't want their customers to be endangered by their sites but at the same time want to remain competitive in this booming market. We learned that more restrictions will cause teens to go somewhere else that has fewer restrictions, with the unintended consequence of increasing their chances of being victimized. We learned that the current age verification technology is ineffective for children too young to appear in public records databases. We learned the increased importance of education messages, and engaging teens to become a part of their own online safety.

We learned that the industry's brightest minds that created this technology in the first place can work together to solve this problem, with the help of policy makers, law enforcement and children's advocacy groups.

The recent concern about social networking sites has given the operators of these sites a clear window of opportunity to take this problem seriously and take action to make their sites safer for children. NCMEC is encouraged by the steps already taken by some of these sites. Myspace has named a new Chief Security Officer, a former federal prosecutor with experience in child exploitation issues. Other sites have demonstrated a similar commitment, and are in the process of changing certain features on their sites that help make children less vulnerable.

These are important first steps, but we strongly urge them to continue their progress by working closely with the various state Attorneys General, law enforcement and others to bring about real change. There is more that can be done and the time to do it is now.

We need to do a better job as a nation of identifying and addressing the greatest risks to our children today. We need to help protect children through education, open dialogue and elevated awareness. By working with industry leaders we can expand our outreach and educate parents, guardians, teens and the general public about this recent technology and ways to ensure safer experiences online.

Reform the Statute of Limitations to Bring Victims Justice

Marci A. Hamilton

Marci A. Hamilton is a professor of public law at New York City's Yeshiva University Benjamin N. Cardozo School of Law and is noted as a leading scholar in the area of First Amendment rights. She has represented clergy abuse survivors on constitutional issues and is the author of God vs. Gavel: Religion and the Rule of Law.

From every tragedy there is something to be learned. The Catholic Church's struggle with sexual abuse of children by members of its clergy is no different. But the lesson is one for the entire country, not just the church.

Although there were inklings of the church's clerical abuse problem before 2002, when *The Boston Globe* began publishing its Pulitzer Prize-winning reports, it was only then that the general public became aware of the scope of the problem.

Two forces worked together to increase the problem: (1) the church shuttled abusing priests among parishes and dioceses with no notice to families and the laity; and (2) the victims of abuse were incapable of coming forward until they had reached a psychologically safe place, often well into adulthood.

The church's actions were indefensible, but its behavior was not unique. Since 2002, one church group after another has been publicly identified with cases of abuse, and victims have come forward from the Jehovah's Witnesses, Southern Baptists, Mormons and Jewish denominations. Sexual abuse

Marci A. Hamilton, "What the Clergy Abuse Crisis Has Taught Us," *America*, vol. 195, no. 8, September 25, 2006, pp. 17–20. Copyright © 2006 americamagazine.org. All rights reserved. Reproduced by permission of America Press. For subscription information, visit http://americamagazine.org.

by members of the clergy—and coverups by religious institutions—are nondenominational.

And the victims' actions were typical of all victims of sexual abuse of children. It takes a certain amount of maturity and perspective to understand what was done to them. Most have to become adults before they can comprehend that their childhood was stolen from them.

The numbers alone are chilling. Nationally, authorities receive reports of child sexual abuse incidents less than 20 percent of the time, with approximately 25 percent of abused girls and 17 percent of boys reporting. As a society, we have plainly failed to offer adequate refuge or justice for these most vulnerable victims.

It is clear: statutes of limitations for sexual abuse of children need to be abolished, as the federal government, Maine, Alaska and Idaho have already done.

It was only when the victims turned to the law that we learned that our society has been cheating abuse victims out of any meaningful justice.

Coming Forward

The problem of limited reporting, which resulted in too little justice, was simple to identify, and it transcended the church's story. Statutes of limitations for sexual abuse of children are so short in most states (sometimes only two years from the date of the assault) that victims of such sexual abuse rarely are able to prosecute or sue for the harm done to them.

It was also a psychological reality that the vast majority could not come forward soon enough. Consequently, the laws weighed heavily in favor of the perpetrators and against the child victims. The system was badly flawed, even corrupt.

In recent years, Americans have been focusing on the recidivism of pedophiles. The resulting reforms have been mani-

fold: the introduction of so-called Megan's laws publicly identifying convicted sex offenders, the creation of databases of
perpetrators of child abuse, the extension of prison sentences
and even the introduction of the death penalty in some states.
But these reforms did not fix the primary problem to which
the church's scandal pointed—the unfairness of the statutes of
limitations for the sexual abuse of children.

Reforming Statutes of Limitation

Because our laws have failed so miserably, reform of statutes
of limitations is needed for all victims, past and present. Although the revelations about the Catholic Church were a cata-
lyst, the law needs to be changed across the board—without
reference to this or any other church, or to any particular
secular organization.

---

*[Temporarily suspending the civil statute of limitations
opens] the door of justice to victims from the past to sue
those who caused them harm.*

The solution needs no task force or further study. It is
clear: statutes of limitations for sexual abuse of children need
to be abolished, as the federal government, Maine, Alaska and
Idaho have already done. Murder has no statute of limitations
because the victim can never speak for himself or herself.
Child abuse, as we have learned, is little different. It involves a
heinous crime, a powerless and vulnerable victim incapable of
speaking for himself or herself and the murder of the victim's
very childhood and soul.

But abolition of the statutes of limitations regarding sexual
abuse of children is helpful only for recent or future victims.
For those victims for whose abuse the statutes of limitations
have expired, for whom the law was so inadequate, there must
be another fix if there is to be any chance for justice. That fix

is "window" legislation, which has already been passed in California and is currently under consideration in about a dozen other states.

The window works as follows: for one or two years, the state legislature suspends the civil statute of limitations on sexual abuse of children, opening the door of justice to victims from the past to sue those who caused them harm. It is straightforward and simple justice.

California tried to create a window for both criminal prosecution and civil lawsuits, but the United States Supreme Court held in a 5-to-4 decision that it was a violation of the Constitution's prohibition of ex post facto laws to suspend the criminal statutes of limitations. As a result, the only way for people who are already victims to obtain any justice, in the wake of our collective failure to protect them, is through a civil litigation window.

Civil Litigation

Civil litigation through such a window is the only way we as a society will learn the monstrous secrets still withheld by so many—perhaps every religious organization, every perpetrator of incest and every adult or organization whose members have sexually assaulted a child or made such an assault possible. Without the due process of the legal system, those secrets will remain buried, perpetrators will remain free to continue molesting (as we have learned from the anti-recidivism movement), and children will be at serious risk. It takes the law to force these secrets into the sunlight.

The primary barriers to legislative reform to aid victims of sexual abuse as children ... are the state Catholic conferences, which lobby state governments.

The most common objection to the window and lengthy statutes of limitations is that evidence will be stale, creating a risk of a miscarriage of justice. Such statutes are most important in cases involving property or business interests, where stability and predictability of ownership are crucial to a stable economy. In contrast, the heinous nature of a personal crime—like murder—often argues against the efficiency and docket-control principles that support a statute of limitations. Anyone who has watched the television show *Cold Case* has seen these principles in action. In those situations, justice—even when delayed—is more valuable to society than mere efficiency. That value is multiplied in the context of sexual abuse of children, where the perpetrator is likely to have many victims over a long period of time. Whenever a perpetrator and his or her enablers are stopped and publicly identified, there is a strong likelihood that future crimes will be prevented.

The window does not alter any of the other rules that ensure a fair trial, including the burdens of proof, rules of evidence and the application of particular privileges. As in all other cases, the older the case, the more difficult the victim's task. But these concerns are overblown in many employment cases, because the evidence is pristinely preserved in the employment histories of the pedophiles involved. Indeed, strenuous objections in church circles to the window arise in no small part, I think, because of fears that revelations that will occur when the church is forced to open confidential archives that still may hide the *identities* of sexual predators.

The most specious legal objection to the window legislation is that it is "targeting the Catholic Church." Nothing is further from the truth. While it is true that the Catholic Church's problems revealed deficiencies in the legal system, there is not a single state proposal that singles out the church. All organizations and individuals responsible for the prevalence of sexual abuse of children are being "targeted." This includes, as we have come to learn, a host of religious organizations, secular organizations and family members. The trigger for the reform may well be the enormity of the church's problems, but the reason for the reform is that the shortness of the time periods allowed by statutes of limitations for sexual abuse of children have been a general blockade to justice and truth.

The Colorado Case

The following may well sound harsh, but it is unfortunately true: The primary barriers to legislative reform to aid victims of sexual abuse as children in the United States are the state Catholic conferences, which lobby state governments.

Most maneuvering by church officials on the state level to prevent window legislation occurs behind closed doors (often before victims even broach the topic), but a public battle occurred in Colorado. Senator Joan Fitzgerald, president of the Colorado Senate, and Representative Gwyn Green introduced legislation in each house addressing the statute of limitations. Fitzgerald (a lifelong Catholic) was staunchly behind window legislation, while Green's bill would have abolished the statute of limitations for sexual abuse of children. Both were deeply upset to learn how many child abuse claims were prematurely shortened by unfair statutes of limitations. Both bills applied to all private entities.

Legislators must amend the statutes of limitations, even if it means additional liability for the church [and other institutions with the same problem].

The Archdiocese of Denver hired an expensive public relations firm and initiated a vigorous attack in the media and from the pulpit. The diocese's public relations firm charged that the bills were "anti-Catholic" and intended to "bankrupt" the church. Following Masses, Catholic parishioners were handed preprinted cards to be signed and sent to state lawmakers. The public relations campaign "proved" the anti-

Catholic bias by pointing out that the bills applied only to private entities. Archbishop Charles Chaput of Denver and his supporters pointed vigorously at the public school system as exempt from the bills. Notwithstanding the fact that private and public entities are almost always addressed in separate legislation, the archbishop scored with his tactics and succeeded in pulling all but two Republicans away from the bills.

The archdiocese did not inform Catholics that public schools had been under a state mandate to report child abuse since at least the early 1980's, while the church had not been required to report until the late 1990's. Moreover, public schools are required to make public any materials relating to child abuse by one of their employees. As Representative Green pointed out recently, archdiocesan representatives made it clear that the church would never agree to divulge any files involving its priests or the abuse of children. The archdiocese opposed the window. It knew from other archdioceses that litigation was the only weapon that could force its secrets into the open.

Catholic conferences in each state often tell the press, laity and politicians that window legislation will "bankrupt" the church, that parishes and schools will be closed and services cut. But Cardinal Sean O'Malley, O.F.M.Cap., . . . disclosed that the settlements in the Archdiocese of Boston came largely from insurance payouts and the sale of nonreligious property. He emphasized that the decline in services in Boston is attributable to the faithful's rebellion against the hierarchy, resulting in their decreased giving, not to payments made by the archdiocese to the victims.

Children an Absolute Priority

Voice of the Faithful recently approved a platform in full support of the window. The time has come for all lay people to demand justice for the victims of their own institution and to make it plain to the hierarchy that as a society we must make children an absolute priority. That means that legislators must amend the statutes of limitations, even if it means additional liability for the church. (The same goes for the many other institutions with the same problem, of which there are plenty.)

The most positive and proactive move Catholics disgusted with the scandal of sexual abuse by members of the clergy can make right now is to let elected representatives know that children must be a top priority, that the laws on the books in most states are inadequate to protect children and that they are far more likely to vote for a representative actively working for the victims of childhood sexual abuse, not for the perpetrators. Silence perpetuates a system that favors abusers and their enablers over abused children.

The sexual abuse crisis in the Catholic Church has the potential to be positively transformative for the United States. We may well be able to move closer to Jesus' command to protect the children from harm—but only if we act on the lessons learned.

The National Sex Offender Public Registry Is a Cost-Effective and Powerful Tool

Regina B. Schofield

Regina B. Schofield is assistant attorney general for the office of Justice Programs in the U.S. Department of Justice.

On July 20, 2005, the U.S. Department of Justice launched the National Sex Offender Public Registry (NSOPR). a searchable Web site that links state and territory sex-offender public registries and allows users access to public information on sex offenders throughout the country.

NSOPR, which currently links to 22 state registries, offers information on almost 200,000 registered sex offenders nationwide. In the coming months, all states will link to the site, giving the public access to information on all 500,000 registered sex offenders in the United States.

NSOPR went live two months after [former] Attorney General Alberto Gonzales directed the U.S. Department Office of Justice Programs (OJP) to design a national site that would link at least 20 state sex-offender public registries and be available for public use in 60 days. Real-time access to public sex offender information, Attorney General Gonzales stressed, is one critical resource to help Americans identify sex offenders beyond their own streets or states. The department exceeded its goal by linking 22 states. In a 12-hour period following its unveiling, the site received 22 million hits—almost 1,000 hits per second.

A single query from any Web-capable computer allows NSOPR to deliver instant matches on sex offenders, including

Regina B. Schofield, "National Sex Offender Public Registry," *Public Management*, vol. 88, no. 1, January 2006, p. 35. Copyright © 2006 International City/County Management Association. Reproduced by permission.

detailed information and often photographs, from state public registries. Mirroring industry standards, the Web services offered and the Justice Department's Global Justice eXtensible Markup Language (XML, a common computer language that standardizes data and facilities data sharing) establish a link between NSOPR and state sex-offender public registries. Users can initiate local, state, and national searches based on a name, zip code, county, city, or town. Plans are in place to furnish additional NSOPR options, especially radius searches and mapping capabilities.

Why the National Offender Registry Works

America's communities have long awaited a national site to search for sex offenders. Nonetheless, the response to the department's newest resource is staggering. A look "behind the screen" reveals three keys to NSOPR's success:

NSOPR was built in partnership with federal, state, and private sector partners. That a national search site was constructed in just 60 days is a tribute to the coordinated efforts of all levels of government, together with the private sector, as they focused on the problem of how to better protect children and communities today—not days or months from now.

NSOPR allows states to maintain control over their own data. States are actively participating in this unprecedented public safety opportunity in large part because they retain control over their public sex-offender data, rather than submitting it to a costly or difficult-to-maintain national repository. By design, once a query has been entered, NSOPR simply "delivers" users to the state site hosting the information.

NSOPR is cost-effective for both citizens and states. Unlike some Web sites that claim to offer national sex-offender information, NSOPR does not require users to submit extensive personal information or to pay a fee to access the information they seek. Equally important, states bear no cost to link to the site, which has cost the Department of Justice and its partners just under $1 million to design and deliver.

Proactive Uses for Technology

NSOPR is in its formative stages. OJP continues to work with states and territories, all of which have indicated their intent to participate, to link them to the site. To ensure the accuracy and timeliness of the data citizens seek, OJP will offer technical assistance to states as they implement and enhance their sex-offender public registries.

From a technology standpoint, NSOPR bandwidth, as well as load capacity, will be added to enlarge the "tunnel" through which queries travel, allowing searches to reach state public sex-offender registries more quickly.

NSOPR currently gives concerned citizens easy-to-use and free access to information on two out of every live registered sex offenders in the United States. Thanks to the National Sex Offender Public Registry, they can now take a proactive and meaningful step in protecting a child's life.

Containment and Surveillance Plus Registries Equals Real Protection

Kim Talman

Kim Talman is the chair of the New York chapter of the National Association to Protect Children (PROTECT). She testified in public hearings on Megan's Law before the New York State Senate's Standing Committee on Crime Victims, Crime and Correction regarding the need to strengthen the state of New York's existing registration policy.

Mr. Chairman, distinguished Senators, thank you for the opportunity to address you today. I am Kim Talman, the New York Chair of the National Association to Protect Children, also known as PROTECT.

PROTECT is a nonpartisan membership association, with members in all 50 states and 9 countries. Our sole focus is on the protection of children from abuse and neglect. We advocate tougher, smarter laws against child abuse and generous help and assistance for child victims.

PROTECT's founders realized that virtually every constituency in America—whether senior citizens, gun owners, teachers or union members—has an organized voice in the political arena, except children. Our mission is to fight for abused and neglected children in the same serious way others fight for their special interests. We stick to the basic, mainstream ideas that the vast majority of Americans can agree on. Since we began less than three years ago, we have worked successfully to pass child protection laws in seven states.

Kim Talman, testimony given before the New York Senate, Standing Committee on Crime Victims, Crime, and Correction: Public Hearings on Megan's Law, www.protect .org, June 7, 2005. Reproduced by permission of the author.

Registration Laws Dispense Much-Needed Information

Since the mid 1990s, the purpose and goals of sex offender databases and registries has changed a great deal.

Sex offender registries . . . are not—even by the most wildly optimistic standards—any kind of substitute for real surveillance, supervision or public safety.

Before "Megan's Law" and the Jacob Wetterling Act, there was the National Child Protection Act of 1993, also known as the "Oprah bill." This legislation was conceived by one of PROTECT's founders, attorney Andrew Vachss, and promoted by television host Oprah Winfrey. It required the states to report criminal indictments and convictions to a federal database, enabling agencies that serve children all across America to have access to national background checks for the first time. While not creating a registry, per se, this Act was an extremely important first step towards protecting children by ensuring that authorities know who potentially dangerous predators are. The fundamental goal of this legislation was a first order of business: *getting information about sex offenders into the hands of those with an immediate need for it, where it could be used in a measurable way to protect children.*

The murder of 11-year-old Jacob Wetterling inspired the Jacob Wetterling Act a year later. This legislation required the states to establish sex offender registries. While public distribution of this information was permitted, it was not required. The primary goal of the Wetterling Act was *getting information about sex offenders into the hands of state and local law enforcement.*

The murder of 7-year-old Megan Kanka led to the enactment of "Megan's Law" in 1996, which told states to open up their registries—at least in part—to the public. Americans were beginning to realize that there was information on these registries they had a powerful reason to know, and they wanted access. The goal of "Megan's Law," therefore was *getting information about sex offenders into the hands of parents, caregivers, families and communities.*

In one way, the increasing distribution of information about convicted sex offenders has had a profound impact on our nation. For the first time in American history, the ugly truth about the rampant sexual abuse of children is nearly impossible to sweep under the rug.

With each passing year from the mid-90's on, the number of convicted sex offenders showing up on public registries has steadily mushroomed. Nine years after "Megan's Law" was passed, there are over half a million registered sex offenders in the U.S. Millions of Americans have now had the unforgettable experience of logging on to the internet to find that sexual offenders are close to home . . . in fact, all around us. And many of us want greater protection for children as a result.

That's the good news.

Registries Are Not a Cure-All

The bad news—to put it bluntly—is that while sex offender registries are cheap, easy, popular and always good for media coverage, *they are not—even by the most wildly optimistic standards—any kind of substitute for real surveillance, supervision or public safety.*

Unfortunately, where the media goes, public policy makers are not far behind.

Please do not misunderstand. PROTECT—and our New York members—believes in sex offender registries. We want parents, grandparents, caregivers and other concerned citizens to have access to them. We commend you for your work to toughen and improve New York's sex offender registry, and we know that you have been working on this for some time.

But in the decade since the passage of "Megan's Law," a very unfortunate thing has happened. Television's obsession with stranger abductions of children—which are a very tiny percentage of all sex crimes against children—fueled the public's fear of child sexual predators. And at the same time, the media began giving a great deal of coverage to sex offender registries, because they hit close to home for the public and are a treasure trove of two things the news media craves: pictures and real life stories.

Unfortunately, where the media goes, public policy makers are not far behind.

When it comes to child sexual abusers, meaningful surveillance and community safety require eyes on the ground.

So, within one decade, what began as an effort to put useful information into the hands of child caregivers, law enforcement and communities *became our foremost national policy for dealing with child sexual abusers*:

- Registering as a sex offender became an actual sentence in and of itself! . . . one often justifying little or no prison time.

- Tougher registration requirements—enacted through perennial "get tough" sex offender bills—became the equivalent of getting tougher on child sexual abuse.

- Giving an unsuspecting public a "heads up!" about a child sexual predator in their neighborhood somehow became a substitute for actually protecting that public.

We should be clear about what we have been telling the public these last nine years about "Megan's Law." The message is: Child molesters on the registry are being watched. You and your family are safer because of it.

Now, with the horrible abduction and murder of little Jessica Lunsford of Florida by a repeat offender named John Couey, we are in danger of departing even further from reality. Whereas first we sought to give the public information about who is a danger and where they are . . . and then we began purporting that registration in and of itself made communities safer . . . now we see new federal legislation proposed that goes one step further: sex offender registries are now talked about as ways to "track" and "monitor" sex offenders, or actually conduct surveillance and impose restrictions.

The most dramatic, media-popular example of this is, of course, the GPS satellite tracking device. This novel technology sounds so serious that it's hard for most Americans not to be impressed and a little excited. Once again, the clear impression the public gets is that we will be all over these guys! Or as Representative Mark Foley said when he . . . introduced legislation with Senator Orrin Hatch: we "will make prey of predators."

Failure to register should be a felony, with mandatory jail or prison sentences for willful or repeat failure to register.

But it just doesn't work that way. Sex offender registries are sex offender registries. They are not a substitute for prison, probation or parole. Eyes in the sky are a great tool for law enforcement. But when it comes to child sexual abusers, meaningful surveillance and community safety require eyes on the ground.

Watch and Contain Predators

What New Yorkers want is very simple: we want individuals who are known by their conduct to be sexually dangerous to children to be removed from society for as long as possible. Then, if and when they are released, we want them contained and under close surveillance for a very long time. Most New Yorkers would agree there are no higher priorities than this.

Let me give you just six examples of meaningful community safeguards against child sexual abusers:

- Prohibit them from living with children.

- Conduct checks on activities and employment where children might be involved.

- Conduct unannounced visits and searches.

- Require mandatory sex offender treatment, whether it works or not.

- Search hard drives for child pornography.

- Have the ability to take law enforcement action if violations are found.

If you tell someone like me, a mother and hardware store owner from Long Island, that a known child molester is being released to my neighborhood, these are the types of protections that I hope you have in mind.

But not one of these things is possible through a sex offender registry program.

In order for the state to have the legal authority to do any of these things, a sex offender must be serving a sentence of probation or parole. Most offenders are on probation or parole a very short period of time, and most registered sex offenders are simply unsupervised. That's the dirty little secret that the public and media don't realize.

But I can assure you as a fairly average New Yorker, I am not that interested in the next John Couey moving in across the street from me with a GPS device on his leg and no supervision or restrictions whatsoever. I would take very little comfort in that, even if I did have the privilege of looking him up on the internet.

The public wants assurance from its leaders that sex offenders released into the community are being closely monitored and restricted.

There will be some who will argue, "Fine. But probation and parole is a separate issue, and we are here to discuss the sex offender registry." The fact is, the sex offender registration and real community supervision have been blurred in the minds of the media, public and most lawmakers. This is primarily the result of policymakers and legislators representing *sex offender registration* as *sex offender management.* It would be a great disservice to compound this problem at a time when the public is desperately seeking assurance from its leaders that they will be protected from released sex offenders. If leaders respond to tragedies resulting from the lack of close surveillance and management of sex offenders—such as the Jessica Lunsford case in Florida—by calling for tougher sex offender registry requirements, then it is incumbent upon them to also take up the real solution: *containment and surveillance.*

Real Management and Law Enforcement

PROTECT has several specific recommendations we would make:

1. *Improve public access to New York's sex offender registry.* We support removing barriers to public access, such as the requirement in New York that citizens provide law enforcement with an exact name and social security or driver's license number in order to access information. This is clearly not in the spirit of "Megan's Law," and, in fact, it seems an example of resistance to that spirit. We also support legislation to ex-

pand internet access to registry information beyond Level 3 offenders, which is a more restrictive policy than we see in many states.

2. Enforce registration seriously. Federal legislation now moving through Congress would push all states towards making failure to register a "strict liability" felony and using GPS tracking devices to locate absconders. These measures have the potential to greatly reduce "failure to register" problems. New York should anticipate these changes and devote sufficient resources towards realizing this goal.

We see common barriers in many states to solving the absconder problem. First, many states have weak "failure to register" laws. Failure to register should be a felony, with mandatory jail or prison sentences for willful or repeat failure to register. States that fail to take this seriously will not only put their citizens at risk, they risk wasting precious law enforcement resources chasing absconders.

The best solution for protecting communities from released sex offenders is . . . utilizing sex offender registries in conjunction with long-term containment and surveillance.

Another common problem is a failure to aggressively prosecute and sentence absconders. Virginia's Criminal Sentencing Commission, for example, found that although penalties of up to five years were on the books for failure to register, fewer than five percent of all absconders were ever convicted. We do not have these estimates for New York, but we recommend that you carefully scrutinize this.

3. Enact lifetime probation or parole, not just lifetime registration. The public wants assurance from its leaders that sex offenders released into the community are being closely monitored and restricted.

Lifetime sex offender registration is a worthwhile goal for many offenders, but without lifetime probation or parole it is virtually toothless. We believe that incapacitation of persons sexually dangerous to children should be the State's paramount goal. If and when these offenders are released, however, they should be on long-term or lifetime probation or parole. This will require statutory changes, so that offenders serve split sentences: a period of confinement followed by long-term or Lifetime community supervision, which can be revoked if the offender fails to comply with conditions. Illinois is one state that has recently embraced this model, combining it with intensive "containment" teams.

4. *Create highly-specialized, well-trained and funded containment and surveillance teams.* Some New York communities have already pioneered specialized probation and parole teams for sex offenders. Specialized probation and parole teams are recognized nationally as the only effective way to monitor, or "manage," sex offenders living in the community. These should exist in every New York community and be well-funded and supported. These are the front-line protectors of children, women and families. No satellite tracking device can do this. GPS tracking cannot tell you if an offender is at home watching television . . . or in a child's bedroom. It does not know if the wearer is out in the yard raking leaves . . . or next door babysitting. And it cannot drop by unannounced, monitor contact with children or intervene before another crime is committed. For that we need dedicated, well-trained human beings.

5. *Use a tougher, better-run Registry in tandem with containment and surveillance.* Ultimately, the best solution for protecting communities from released sex offenders is a two-pronged approach, utilizing sex offender registries in conjunction with long-term containment and surveillance. This is the only responsible path if dangerous child sexual abusers are going to be returned to live among an unsuspecting public.

Stop the Trend of Ineffective Legislation

New reports are getting more frequent each month about local communities struggling desperately to cope with sex offenders in their midst. Municipal governments are attempting to zone sex offenders right out of town. Individual citizens are posting fliers and notifying neighbors. Offenders have been ordered to put signs in their yards.

None of these things should be happening. They are occurring because our laws and our criminal justice system are not taking the problem of sexual predators seriously. If and when convicted child sexual abusers are released from prison, they should be released to long-term probation or parole, under the close supervision of specialized sex offender teams.

That takes money and resources. Whether and how well we do it is the measure of our commitment to protecting children and safeguarding New York families.

Targeting Offenders' Re-entry into Society and Community Education Are Key

Deborah Donovan Rice

Deborah Donovan Rice is the director of public policy for the national nonprofit organization Stop It Now!, which is dedicated to preventing child sexual abuse using a public health approach; she is also an expressive arts therapist, and a member of the National Coalition for the Prevention of Child Sexual Exploitation.

In the absence of an informed public debate on the re-entry of those who have been convicted of sex crimes, fear-based laws are being enacted across the country. Recent trends have made community re-entry the trigger point for society's most venomous and simplistic responses toward people with a history of sexually offending. Ironically, the re-entry process also has the potential to become one of the best forums for creating the conditions for a safer community and preventing the sexual abuse of children.

Public Debate Needed

Typical conversations about sexual abuse in the media or on the streets condemn child sexual abuse as a horrendous crime and misdeed, often taking a prejudicial turn so sharp as to create conditions for vigilantism and murder. Media adds to this divisive atmosphere by emphasizing the rarest type of sexual deviance. The widespread impact of current laws on offenders themselves and their family members is usually overlooked or absent in news coverage, an oversight that works against community interest. [According to Amy and David

Deborah Donovan Rice, "Community Re-entry Recast as Primary Prevention," *Sex Offender Law Report*, vol. 7, no. 5, August/September 2006, pp. 65, 78–80. Copyright © 2006 Civic Research Institute, Inc. Reproduced by permission.

Goodman, in their book The Exception to the Rulers: Exposing Oily Politicians, War Profiteers, and the Media That Love Them:]

Change starts with ordinary people working in their communities. And that's where media should start as well. The role of the media isn't to agree with any person or group—or the government or the powerful. But the media do have a responsibility to include all voices in the discourse. Then let the people decide.

Embedded Assumptions Not Supported by Scientific Evidence

In many instances, the general public and policy-makers continue to hold beliefs that are not based on the current research. As a result, laws have several assumptions embedded in them that impact re-entry negatively and are not supported by the scientific evidence. Dr. Fred Berlin, director of the National Institute for the Study, Prevention, and Treatment of Sexual Trauma, states:

Much of public policy today in this area is based on the exception rather than the rule—those horrible cases where there is a kidnapping, a sexual assault, and a murder of a young child. That is a fraction of 1% of the big problem.

As a culture, we have historically opted for silence and denial rather than to educate ourselves with accurate information about child sexual abuse.

The lack of knowledge about who offends needs to be countered with the fact that approximately 60% of boys and 80% of girls who are sexually victimized are abused by someone known to the child or the child's family.

Vermont's Experience with Stop It Now!

Vermont's experience with Megan's Law in 1996 offers a powerful example of how well intentioned policy initiatives negatively impact prevention efforts. Stop It Now!, founded in

1992, is a national nonprofit organization that introduced a groundbreaking public health approach to prevent the sexual abuse of children. Its public policy, public education, and research programs emphasize adult and community responsibility in prevention. Stop It Now!, along with its Vermont partner, the Safer Society Foundation, Inc., launched the Stop It Now! Vermont program in September 1995. A social marketing campaign and community education were combined with the resource of a helpline for adults who were concerned about their own or someone else's sexual behavior. The helpline was launched in the summer of 1996; in the first six weeks of operation almost 60% of the calls were from people concerned about their sexual thoughts or behaviors. During week seven, news of Megan's Law hit the popular press in Vermont; within a week, the number of calls from abusers or people at-risk to abuse trickled down to zero. Over the intervening years, the number of calls from those seeking help for themselves has increased to approximately 8% of the calls.

Creating the conditions for openness about sexually disordered and sexually exploitive behavior includes addressing the need for factual information.

Recent Trends in Context

As a culture, we have historically opted for silence and denial rather than to educate ourselves with accurate information about child sexual abuse or even about sexuality in general. The current vituperative and punitive tone evidenced in the media and policy discussions begs the question of whether or not those with sexual behavior problems feel they can come forward and seek help.

So what are the critical steps that might help prevent the sexual abuse of children?

Tony Ward and Mark Brown state, "The best way to lower recidivism rates is to equip individuals with the tools to live more fulfilling lives." They further stated, "At the end of the day, most offenders have more in common with us than not, and like the rest of humanity have needs to be loved, valued, to function competently, and to be part of a community." While criminal justice solutions could provide a foundation for creating community safety, a combination of prevention activities, risk management, and a positive approach to treatment increases the likelihood of successful re-entry for the individual returning to the community. Such a paradigm shift would create new opportunities for the primary prevention of sexual abuse.

Creating Conditions for Primary Prevention of Child Sexual Abuse

Every day on our helpline, we hear about the real barriers that stop well-intentioned, nonoffending adults from taking action before a child is victimized. We have come to understand that we adults have a stake in ignoring abuse. We need to hold ourselves as a community, accountable, as well as the people who offend, for our failure to address these contributing factors. By being accountable for sharing the responsibility for creating a safer environment, there is a role for each community member to play in preventing future sexual assaults whether as a private citizen or as a public official.

Courage to Disturb the Surface

Stop It Now!'s research has shown that although the public is aware of child sexual abuse, most people simply do not know what to do about it. Most people in today's society lack a frame of reference for talking about child sexual abuse. Recognizing the educational potential of introducing real faces into a normally abstract discussion about the effects of child sexual abuse, Stop It Now! created a public Dialogue Project by gathering a panel of people who have been personally affected by sexual abuse—survivors, recovering sex offenders, and their family members. The dialogue participants are able to model an honest conversation about the potentials and the challenges to preventing the sexual abuse of a child. Describing her experience with the Dialogue Project, one survivor of child sexual abuse noted that having an authentic conversation about abuse requires the "courage to disturb the surface, to let go of appearances, and to disrupt normal social relations." "Let's Talk" is a companion publication on how to talk about child sexual abuse and is also articulated in the trainer module.

Need for Factual Information

Creating the conditions for openness about sexually disordered and sexually exploitive behavior includes addressing the need for factual information. To that end, Stop It Now! publications offer facts about those who commit child sexual abuse and information about what individuals can do to prevent or stop sexual abuse. A third publication answers the question, "Do Children Sexually Abuse Other Children?" All three publications could also serve as take-home materials for adults participating in community education meetings and can be downloaded or ordered in hard copy form. For those who are asking the question about what to do if a sex offender moves into the neighborhood, "Creating a Family Safety Plan" offers additional information.

Public education is a critical first step in protecting children from child sexual abuse.

The state-by-state sex offender registries were meant to assist law enforcement and probation and parole officers in the supervision of those who have been convicted of sex crimes, not to create conditions of greater danger to community members. The recent murders in Maine of two men listed on the state sex offender registry list underscore the need for reconsidering how the registry and community notification is to be used.

Public Education Is Critical First Step

The Georgia legislature's . . . passage of harsh new restrictions on registered sex offenders prompted Stop It Now! Georgia's statewide coordinator, Sally Thigpen, to observe:

> Public education is a critical first step in protecting children from child sexual abuse. HB1059, in addition to the overbroad application of increased restrictions and penalties, is missing critical opportunities to incorporate public education into the practice of public access to registrant information . . . When the public seeks information about registered sex offenders, they should also be given information about certain realities:
>
> - Most children who are, or who will be, sexually abused will not be abused by someone on the sex offender registry. In fact, over 90% of children who are, or will be, sexually abused will be abused by someone they know and trust—most likely someone within their own family.
>
> - A vast majority—up to 88%—of child sexual abuse is never reported. While the registry offers communities important information, it does not include most individuals who pose a risk to sexually abused children.
>
> - The low rate of reporting leads to the conclusion that the approximate 265,000 convicted sex offenders under the authority of corrections agencies in the United States represent less than 10% of all sex offenders living in communities nationwide.
>
> Coupling current policy efforts with components of public education—for example, a link on the web-based registry to

sources of information about the prevention of the perpetration of child sexual abuse—would go a long way to comprehensively inform the public about the issue of child sexual abuse and the options to protect children effectively—before a child is harmed.

Provide Information Proactively

Recasting community notification meetings as community education meetings offers another opportunity to provide information proactively, rather than using the re-entry of a specific offender into the community as a starting place for a conversation. Detective Robert A. Shilling, Jr., lead detective in the Seattle Police Department's Sex and Kidnapping Offender unit, describes key components of his program: countering societal myths with facts, multidisciplinary team presentation, and positive messages about the role of community members in the re-entry process. Examples of the messages include:

> Community members have a vested interest in the success of the returning ex-offender, because their failure means we have another victim which is unacceptable to everyone; most offenders want people to know and this is viewed as a support to stay on the straight and narrow, as a neighbor knows who they are and what they've done. Be vigilant, but leave them alone and let them get on with their life.

It takes all adult community members to create the conditions for safety by educating themselves about child sexual abuse.

"These public education meetings are conducted citywide by neighborhoods utilizing schools. Meeting notices are sent to parents via the schools as well as being published in local newspapers." This level of community education enables adults to learn enough to begin to prevent forum abuse.

Community Forum Component

The New York Coalition of Sex Offender Management has instituted a comprehensive, evidence-based approach which integrates best practice information from the Center for Sex Offender Management and research on prosocial and procriminal criminogenic needs. This victim-centered initiative involves a victim service provider, citizen/survivor, law enforcement, district attorney, public defender, probation/parole, and sex offender treatment provider in a steering committee. One of the fundamental components is the community forum, designed to educate the community and minimize unrealistic expectations. These two-hour forums begin with brief panel presentations across disciplines followed by questions and discussion.

Target Those at Highest Risk

Circles of Support and Accountability (COSA) offers another approach, targeting those without aftercare plans and at the highest risk of reoffense. COSA seeks to "substantially reduce the risk of future sexual victimization of community members by assisting and supporting released men in their task of integrating with the community and leading responsible, productive, and accountable lives." An ex-offender known as the Core Member and five community volunteers comprise an inner circle of support. Community-based professionals comprise an outer circle of support for the Core Member and the inner circle in its work. Community members joining with former offenders and professionals can make a difference as evidenced by the results reported: Offenders participating in COSA had a 70% reduction in sexual recidivism.

Cooperative Process
of Shared Responsibility

Whose responsibility is it to assure safe integration of the sex offender into the community? It takes all adult community members to create the conditions for safety by educating themselves about child sexual abuse.

- On a societal level: When judges assign conditions of parole/probation are they informed by best practice for sex offender management?

- For policymakers: Asking the question whether a policy increases or decreases community safety and then looking to the evidence of what is most effective can increase the conditions for community safety. An example would be insuring opportunities for adequate housing and work for former offenders to be able to establish stable lifestyles.

- For the former sex offender: Is there specialized, sex-specific treatment available in the community?

- For professionals: Did re-entry planning begin at the early stage of incarceration? Are pre-release, transition, and community re-entry plans coordinated? Are re-entry plans revised to keep up with changes in circumstances of the offender?

- For the general public: Are there opportunities to educate themselves about preventing sexual abuse?

Putting a human face on child sexual abuse through community education meetings as previously described can move the public discussion to one that is more reasoned and effective in preventing the sexual abuse of children. By participating in steering committees and panels to design and implement this type of forum, community professionals and citizens model sharing the responsibility of creating a safer community.

At its best, community re-entry becomes a cooperative process with a role for all of us to play in preventing future sexual assaults, whether as a private citizen, a public official, or agency professional. True primary prevention demands that each of us be accountable for educating ourselves with a clear understanding of the facts, so we can take the necessary actions in our personal and professional lives to prevent the sexual abuse and sexual exploitation of children.

Organizations to Contact

The editors have compiled the following list of organizations concerned with the issues debated in this book. The descriptions are derived from materials provided by the organizations. All have publications or information available for interested readers. The list was compiled on the date of publication of the present volume; the information provided here may change. Be aware that many organizations take several weeks or longer to respond to inquiries, so allow as much time as possible.

Association for the Treatment of Sexual Abusers (ATSA)
4900 S.W. Griffith Drive, Suite 274, Beaverton, OR 97005
(503) 643-1023 • fax: (503) 643-5084
email: atsa@atsa.com
Web site: www.atsa.com

ATSA is a nonprofit, international organization that was founded to foster research, facilitate informational exchange, further professional education and provide for the advancement of professional standards and practices in the field of sex offender evaluation and treatment. ATSA aims to eliminate sexual victimization, protect communities, and prevent sexual assault through effective, responsible, and ethical treatment of sex offenders, and maintain high standards of professionalism and integrity within its membership. ATSA publishes numerous informational packages, position papers on public policies related to the treatment and management of sex offenders, book and video reviews, and the journal *Sexual Abuse: A Journal of Research and Treatment.*

Center for Sex Offender Management (CSOM)
8403 Colesville Road, Suite 720, Silver Spring, MD 20910
(301) 589-9383 • fax: (301) 589-3505
e-mail: askcsom@csom.org
Web site: www.csom.org

CSOM is a national project that supports state and local jurisdictions in the effective management of sex offenders under community supervision. CSOM's primary goal is to enhance public safety by preventing further victimization through improving the management of sex offenders in the community. CSOM offers numerous publications on its Web site regarding facts on sex offenders and sex offender management, public policies, special offender populations, and offender treatment.

Generation Five (Gen5)
2 Massasoit Street, San Francisco, CA 94110
(415) 285-6658 • fax: (415) 285-6668
e-mail: info@generationfive.org
Web site: www.generationfive.org

Gen5 programs provide leadership training to communities and foster national strategy and information exchange on child sexual abuse. Gen5 is not a direct service organization; rather, they work in collaboration with service providers to ensure that affordable, culturally relevant support is available to survivors, offenders, and affected families.

The Jacob Wetterling Foundation
33 Minnesota Street, PO Box 639, St. Joseph, MN 56374
(320) 363-0470 • fax: (320) 363-0473
e-mail: info@jwf.org
Web site: www.jwf.org

The Jacob Wetterling Foundation is a nonprofit organization that has worked to find missing children and educate children, teens, parents, caregivers, and teachers about personal safety. The foundation fights for stronger laws to protect children from sexual exploitation and takes a close look at repeat sex offenders and how they are managed in Minnesota and nationwide.

Mothers Against Sexual Predators At Large (MASPAL)
P.O. Box 7247, Missoula, MT 59807-9395
e-mail: contact@maspal.org

Web site: www.maspal.org

MASPAL believes there is a connection between the rising numbers of missing children and the rising numbers of known sex offenders and is dedicated to education and legislation for the public regarding this perceived connection. MASPAL works to persuade lawmakers to create pre-release centers in every state to deal with the special concerns of sex offenders, and increase supervision of those individuals after their time has been served. MASPAL also offers an online peer-counseling discussion forum for victims and their families and assists citizens in locating sexual predators living in their communities.

National Alliance to End Sexual Violence (NAESV)
(202) 289-3903
e-mail: efern@wpllc.net
Web site: www.naesv.org

NAESV's board of directors consists of leaders of state sexual assault coalitions and national law, policy, and tribal experts who promote the organization's mission to advance and strengthen public policy on behalf of state coalitions, individuals, and other entities working to end sexual violence. NAESV advocates on behalf of women, children, and men who have been sexually victimized, and utilizes a comprehensive grassroots communication network to shape national policy related to sexual violence and victims' needs, ensure funding for rape crisis programs and sexual assault coalitions, and provide expertise to governments, businesses, and non-profit organizations addressing sexual violence in all of its forms.

National Association to Protect Children (PROTECT)
46 Haywood St., Suite 315, Asheville, NC   28801
(828) 350-9350
e-mail: info@protect.org
Web site: www.protect.org

PROTECT is a national pro-child, anticrime membership association founded on the belief that parents, citizens, and human beings in general have as their first priority the protection of children from harm. PROTECT is committed to building a powerful, nonpartisan force for the protection of children from abuse, exploitation, and neglect and believes that this must be done through a determined single-issue focus, a meaningful mainstream agenda and the use of proven modern political strategies. Members and supporters of PROTECT have written a variety of policy statements and articles, including "Stakes Couldn't Be Higher—Safe Day Care in a Dangerous World" by David Hechler and "What Are You Going to Do About Child Abuse?" by Andrew Vachss.

National Institute for the Study, Prevention and Treatment of Sexual Trauma
104 E. Biddle St., Baltimore, MD   21202
(410) 539-166
Web site: www.fredberlin.com

In 1991, while continuing his work at Johns Hopkins with inpatients manifesting sexual disorders, Dr. Fred Berlin established the National Institute as a free-standing private clinic, which now provides care to patients with a variety of sexual disorders as well as to victims of sexual trauma. The institute is also dedicated to the goal of learning more about prevention by learning more about offenders and their afflictions and helping those who have been sexually traumatized. Services offered include comprehensive psychiatric and forensic evaluations and consultations, individual, group, and family therapy, pharmacotherapy, as well as seminars for professionals and the public.

National Sexual Violence Resource Center (NSVRC)
123 North Enola Dr., Enola, PA   17025
(717) 909-0710 • fax: (717) 909-0714
e-mail: resources@nsvrc.org
Web site: www.nsvrc.org

NSVRC is a national information and resource hub relating to all aspects of sexual violence, is a project of the Pennsylvania Coalition Against Rape, and is funded through a grant from the Centers for Disease Control and Prevention's Division of Violence Prevention. NSVRC staff collects and disseminates a wide range of resources on sexual violence including statistics, research, position statements, statutes, training curricula, prevention initiatives and program information to assist coalitions, advocates and others interested in understanding and eliminating sexual violence. NSVRC publishes a semiannual newsletter, *The Resource*, issues press releases and talking points on current events, and coordinates an annual national sexual assault awareness month (SAAM) campaign in April.

Rape, Abuse & Incest National Network (RAINN)
2000 L Street NW, Suite 406, Washington, DC   20036
(202) 544-1034 • fax: (202) 544-3556
e-mail: info@rainn.org
Web site: www.rainn.org

RAINN is a national anti–sexual assault organization that, among its programs, operates the National Sexual Assault Hotline, a nationwide partnership of more than 1,100 local rape treatment hotlines to provide victims of sexual assault with free, confidential services around the clock. RAINN partners with numerous organizations to disseminate information about sexual assault prevention, recovery, and prosecution, and is a frequent resource for television, radio, and print news outlets, as well as local, state, and national policy makers, law enforcement, and rape treatment professionals, on the issues related to rape and sexual assault. RAINN utilizes entertainment industry and community-based relationships to provide pamphlets to young women and men at concerts, on campus, and in communities.

SOhopeful International
1900 NE 181st Ave., Suite 111, Portland, OR   97230
(212) 714-7061

e-mail: info@sohopeful.org
Web site: www.sohopeful.org

SOhopeful is an international civil rights organization, focused on the human, civil, and constitutional rights of sex offenders and their families. SOhopeful does not condone or advocate abuse or excuse offenders, and advocates and encourages offenders to take personal responsibility, seek and participate in treatment, reunite with their families, and reintegrate into the community as active, contributing members of society. SOhopeful seeks to develop relationships with legislators who craft and approve laws dealing with penal codes, convey which provisions they oppose and support, as well as offer alternatives to existing laws mandating such activities as ongoing supervision and lifetime punishment of sex offenders. SOhopeful dispenses information to the public, treatment professionals, and legislators regarding research statistics on recidivism, risk-levels, and the effects of registration and other public policies on offenders and their families.

Stop It Now!
351 Pleasant Street, Suite B319, Northampton, MA   01060
(413) 587-3500 • fax: (413) 587-3505
e-mail: info@stopitnow.org
Web site: www.stopitnow.org

Stop It Now! is a national public health–based organization working to prevent child sexual abuse by educating adults—including those at risk for abusing and their families and friends—about the ways to prevent child sexual abuse and by promoting policy changes at local and national levels to support prevention strategies.

Survivors Network of those Abused by Priests (SNAP)
P.O. Box 6416, Chicago, IL   60680-6416
Toll free: (877) 762-7432
e-mail: SNAPClohessy@aol.com
Web site: www.snapnetwork.org

SNAP is a national support group—with no connections to church or church officials—offering confidential services for women and men victimized by religious authority figures such as priests, ministers, bishops, deacons, and nuns. SNAP offers support in person via monthly self-help group meetings in chapters across the country, over the phone, online, and at twice-a-year national meetings.

Bibliography

Books

Howard E. Barbaree and William L. Marshall, eds.
The Juvenile Sex Offender. 2nd Edition. New York: The Guilford Press, 2006.

Mark Brown
Dangerous Offenders: Punishment and Social Order. New York: Routledge, 2000.

Sarah Brown
Treating Sex Offenders: An Introduction to Sex Offender Treatment Programmes. Portland, OR: Willan Publishing, 2005.

Shawna Cleary
Sex Offenders and Self-Control: Explaining Sexual Violence. New York: LFB Scholarly Publishing, LLC, 2004.

Cathy Cobley
Sex Offenders: Law, Policy, and Practice. 2nd Edition. Bristol, England: Jordans, 2005.

Jacki Craissati
Managing High Risk Sex Offenders in the Community. New York: Brunner-Routledge, 2004.

Robert Geffner, Ph.D., Kristina Crumpton Franey, Psy.D., Teri Geffner Arnold, MSSW, and Robert Falconer, MA, eds.
Identifying and Treating Sex Offenders: Current Approaches, Research, and Techniques. Binghamton, NY: The Haworth Maltreatment & Trauma Press, 2003.

Jake Goldenflame   *Overcoming Sexual Terrorism: 60 Ways to Protect Your Children from Sexual Predators.* New York: iUniverse, Inc., 2006.

Dennis Howitt and Kerry Sheldon   *Sex Offenders and the Internet.* Hoboken, NJ: John Wiley & Sons, Ltd., 2007.

Kirsty Hudson   *Offending Identities: Sex Offenders' Perspectives on Their Treatment and Management.* Portland, OR: Willan Publishing, 2005.

Philip Jenkins   *Moral Panic: Changing Concepts of the Child Molester in America.* New Haven, CT: Yale University Press, 1998.

John Q. La Fond   *Preventing Sexual Violence: How Society Should Cope with Sex Offenders.* Washington, DC: American Psychological Association, 2005.

Amanda Matravers   *Sex Offenders in the Community: Managing and Reducing the Risks.* Portland, OR: Willan, 2003.

Anne-Marie McAlinden   *The Shaming of Sexual Offenders: Risk, Retribution, and Reintegration.* Oxford and Portland, OR: Hart, 2007.

George B. Palermo and Mary Ann Farkas   *The Dilemma of the Sexual Offender.* Springfield, IL: C.C. Thomas, 2001.

R. A. Prentky, Eric S. Janus, and Michael C. Seto
Sexually Coercive Behavior: Understanding and Management. New York: New York Academy of Sciences, 2003.

Anna C. Salter, Ph.D.
Predators: Pedophiles, Rapists, and Other Sex Offenders: Who They Are, How They Operate, and How We Can Protect Ourselves and Our Children. New York: Basic Books, 2003.

Karen J. Terry
Sexual Offenses and Offenders: Theory, Practice, and Policy. Belmont, CA: Thomson Wadsworth, 2006.

Bruce J. Winick and John Q. La Fond, eds.
Protecting Society from Sexually Dangerous Offenders: Law, Justice, and Therapy. Washington, DC: American Psychological Association, 2003.

Periodicals

Ed Asher
"Sex Offender Law Worries Some Victim Groups," *Albuquerque Tribune* (New Mexico), May 1, 2003.

Jim Atkinson
"The Pedophile Next Door," *Texas Monthly*, March 2004.

Daniel Bergner
"The Making of a Molester," *New York Times Magazine*, January 23, 2005.

Scott Christianson
"Barred for Life: Sex Offenders Need Education and Treatment, Not a Lifetime of Civil Lockup," *Times Union* (Albany, NY), January 22, 2006.

Robert Crowe	"Expert: Castration No Cure for Pedophilia," *Houston Chronicle*, May 10, 2005.
Avery Dulles	"Rights of Accused Priests," *America*, June 21–28, 2004.
Kurt Eichenwald	"On the Web, Pedophiles Extend Their Reach," *New York Times*, August 21, 2006.
Gary A. Enos	"Finding a Place for Sex Offenders," *Behavioral Healthcare*, September 2006.
David Finkelhor and Lisa M. Jones	"Explanations for the Decline in Child Sexual Abuse Cases," *Juvenile Justice Bulletin*, January 2004.
James Alan Fox	"Sentiment No Base for Sensible Laws," *Boston Herald*, September 26, 2005.
Brian Friel	"Administration: The War on Kiddie Porn," *National Journal*, March 25, 2006.
Elizabeth Garfinkle	"Coming of Age in America: The Misapplication of Sex-Offender Registration and Community-Notification Laws to Juveniles," *California Law Review*, January 2003.
Danny Hakim	"Debate Pits Public Safety against Sex Felons' Rights," *New York Times*, November 19, 2005.
Anita Hamilton	"Banning the Bad Guys," *Time*, September 5, 2005.

Stacey Hannem and Michael Petrunik — "Canada's Circles of Support and Accountability: A Community Justice Initiative for High-Risk Sex Offenders," *Corrections Today*, December 2004.

Bret R. Hobson — "Banishing Acts: How Far May States Go to Keep Convicted Sex Offenders Away from Children?" *Georgia Law Review*, Spring 2006.

Katy Kelly — "To Protect the Innocent," *U.S. News & World Report*, June 13, 2005.

Timothy F. Kirn — "Sexual-Abuse Cycle Can Be Broken, Experts Assert," *Family Practice News*, July 1, 2006.

Jeffrey Kluger — "What Do Pedophiles Deserve?" *Time*, October 11, 2006.

Wendy Koch — "Sex-Offender Residency Laws Get Second Look," *USA Today*, February 26, 2007.

John Q. La Fond and Bruce J. Winick — "Doing More Than Their Time," *New York Times*, May 21, 2006.

Dahlia Lithwick — "Vile, Vile Pedophile," *Slate.com*, January 7, 2004. www.slate.com.

Donna Lyons — "Where on Earth Are Sex Offenders?" *State Legislatures*, March 2006.

Lisa Madigan — "Get Serious about Sex Offender Registration," *Christian Science Monitor*, February 17, 2004.

Douglas McCollam | "The Shame Game," *Columbia Journalism Review*, January/February 2007. www.cjr.org.

Martha T. Moore | "Sex Crimes Break the Lock on Juvenile Records," *USA Today*, July 10, 2006.

Andrew Murr | "Holes in the Safety Net: A Startling Number of Sex Offenders Are off The Grid," *Newsweek*, February 24, 2003.

New York Times | "Sex Offenders in Exile," December 30, 2006.

Bill O'Reilly | "Justice System Favors Sex Offenders, Not Children," *Chicago Sun-Times*, May 10, 2005.

Page Rockwell | "No Punishment Too Severe?" *Salon.com*, October 31, 2006. www.salon.com.

Jane Ruffin | "Treatment Takes a Lot of Time, Work," *News & Observer* (Raleigh, NC), June 18, 2006.

Charles L. Scott, MD and Trent Holmberg, MD | "Castration of Sex Offenders: Prisoners' Rights versus Public Safety," *Journal of the American Academy of Psychiatry and the Law*, December 2003.

Charles Sheehan | "Sex Offenders Slip Away: For Lack of Housing, Some Spend Parole in Prison, Then Vanish," *Chicago Tribune*, March 31, 2006.

Natalie Singer   "'Stranger Danger' Emphasis Misguided," *Seattle Times*, May 23, 2006.

Meghan
Stromberg   "Locked Up, Then Locked Out," *Planning*, January 2007.

Andrew Vachss   "The Difference between 'Sick' and 'Evil'," *Parade*, July 14, 2002.

Index